The Life Cycles of the Council
on Environmental Quality and the
Environmental Protection Agency

The Life Cycles of the Council on Environmental Quality and the Environmental Protection Agency

1970–2035

JAMES K. CONANT

AND

PETER J. BALINT

Oxford University Press is a department of the University of Oxford. It furthers the University's objective of excellence in research, scholarship, and education by publishing worldwide. Oxford is a registered trade mark of Oxford University Press in the UK and certain other countries.

Published in the United States of America by Oxford University Press
198 Madison Avenue, New York, NY 10016, United States of America

Library of Congress Cataloging-in-Publication Data
Names: Conant, James K., author. | Balint, Peter J., 1950– author.
Title: The life cycles of the Council on Environmental Quality and the
  Environmental Protection Agency : 1970–2035 / James K. Conant and Peter J.
  Balint.
Description: Oxford ; New York, NY : Oxford University Press, [2016] |
  Includes bibliographical references and index.
Identifiers: LCCN 2015032488| ISBN 9780190203702 (hardcover : alk. paper) |
  ISBN 9780190203719 (pbk. : alk. paper)
Subjects: LCSH: Environmental policy—United States. | United States.
  National Environmental Policy Act of 1969. | Council on Environmental
  Quality (U.S.) | United States. Environmental Protection Agency.
Classification: LCC GE180 .C658 2016 | DDC 363.7/05610973—dc23 LC record available at
http://lccn.loc.gov/2015032488

9 8 7 6 5 4 3 2 1

Printed in Canada by Webcom

In Memory of John W. Gaston, Jr.

Whose visionary leadership of the Water Resources and Hazardous Waste Divisions in New Jersey's Department of Environmental Protection during the 1980s provided the inspiration for this book.

J.K.C.

To Judy

P.J.B.

CONTENTS

CONTENTS

PREFACE AND ACKNOWLEDGMENTS

In the U.S. governmental system, executive branch agencies are assigned the duty of implementing legislation passed by Congress and signed into law by the president. Consequently, whether a public law is successfully implemented will depend in part on the health, vitality, and even survival (life cycle) of the agency or agencies assigned to implement it. In this book, we present a life cycle study of the Council on Environmental Quality (CEQ) and the Environmental Protection Agency (EPA). These two agencies are assigned the task of implementing a variety of laws designed to protect the environment and human health. The CEQ was created in the National Environmental Policy Act of 1969 (NEPA), which was signed into law on January 1, 1970. The EPA was created by President Richard Nixon in Reorganization Plan No. 3, which was submitted to Congress in July 1970.

The development of this book was a multiyear collaboration in which each author made equal contributions to the final product. This book manuscript incorporates the work on the CEQ and EPA we had published in two previous journal articles; it also contains a substantially expanded version of the work contained in those articles. In developing this book we drew upon the literatures of public administration, organization theory, public policy, political science, and environmental politics and policy—and we think we make a useful contribution to each of them.

The intellectual origins of this book date back to the 1980s, when Conant was teaching environmental politics and policy at Rutgers

University and, later, public management at New York University. During
that time period, Conant had two articles published on the life cycles of
executive branch organizations in state government: "The Changing Face
of the New Jersey Department of Environmental Protection" and "Stability, Change and Leadership in State Administration: 1970–1986."[1] The first
article evolved from Conant's work with John W. Gaston, Jr., Director of
the Division of Water Resources in the New Jersey's Department of Environmental Protection. Specifically, Conant wrote "The Changing Face of
the New Jersey Department of Environmental Protection" to serve as a resource in both the management education and training program and the
strategic planning process Gaston asked him to develop for the Division.

When Gaston was appointed Assistant Commissioner for Hazardous
Waste, he asked Conant to duplicate the work he had done in Water Resources. As that work was under way, Conant was invited to work with
the Air Quality Division and the Science and Policy Division in the New
Jersey Department of Environmental Protection. In each of these assignments, Conant got a hands-on education in the implementation of pollution control laws that was an essential element to the formulation and
writing of this book.

In 2008, as the fortieth anniversaries of the CEQ and EPA approached,
Conant developed a research plan for a life cycle study of the two agencies. He asked departmental colleague Peter Balint for feedback on the
plan, and, after several conversations about the project, Conant invited
Balint to join him in the study.

Balint came to the project with a research agenda focusing primarily on natural resource management. In the early 2000s, he and several
colleagues, with a grant from the U.S. Forest Service, began a study of
that agency's struggles to manage national forests effectively within an
increasingly polarized political environment. In doing so Balint and
his colleagues delved into the research on so-called wicked problems—
dilemmas characterized by uncertain science, poorly understood risks,
and divergent public values. This work, which led to a book titled *Wicked
Environmental Problems: Managing Uncertainty and Conflict*,[2] strengthened Balint's interest in U.S. government agencies. Balint also brought

to our project on the CEQ and EPA skills in quantitative analysis and knowledge of the history of U.S. environmental policymaking.

The authors want to thank the four research assistants who made valuable contributions to this book: Chris Ford, Mary Weigand, Matt Critchfield, and Kevin Grant.

Conant provided the funding for and supervised the data collection, literature review, and data analysis conducted by Ford, Weigand, and Critchfield. Balint supervised Grant's work on the EPA data.

We also want to thank others who provided assistance with the development of our work. Departmental colleagues Tim Conlan and Pris Reagan provided comments on the initial draft of the CEQ manuscript. The funding for research assistant Kevin Grant's work was authorized by departmental colleagues Colin Dueck and Pris Regan. Scott Keeter of PEW Research and departmental colleagues Gerry Bushee and Rob McGrath offered suggestions on the quantitative methods we employed in our study of the EPA. Keeter also provided excellent counsel on the collection and interpretation of public opinion data.

Jim Burroughs, Matt Chritchfield, Bob Evanson, Lance Miller, John Trela, and Lee Talbot made helpful comments on one or more of the chapters in this book. Talbot, a renowned conservationist who served as chief science advisor at the CEQ in the 1970s, also gave us valuable information about that agency's early years. Susan E. Conant made useful editorial suggestions on Chapters 1 through 4 and 6, and Jennifer Lee Conant provided assistance with various figures and tables in Chapters 3, 4, and 6. Judith Balint made valuable comments on several draft chapters.

We are especially grateful to Angela Chnapko, the Political Science Editor at Oxford University Press, for accepting our book proposal and working with us to bring this book to completion. We also want to thank Oxford University Press's anonymous reviewers for their suggestions on the book proposal and the book manuscript. Their input significantly improved the final product.

Finally, we want to thank two publishers for granting us permission to use material included in Chapters 4 and 5 that was previously published in journal articles. The first article is James K. Conant and Peter J. Balint.

"The Council on Environmental Quality at 40: A Life Cycle Analysis," Environmental Practice 13, no. 2 (2011): 113–21. Copyright © 2011 National Association of Environmental Professionals. Permission granted by Cambridge University Press. The second article is Peter J. Balint and James K. Conant. "The Environmental Protection Agency's Budget from 1970–2010: A Lifecycle Analysis," Public Budgeting and Finance 33, no 4, (2013): 22–42. Copyright © 2013 Public Financial Publications, Inc. Permission granted by John Wiley and Sons.

The Life Cycles of the Council
on Environmental Quality and the
Environmental Protection Agency

Environmental Politics, Policy, and Administration in the United States

A variety of human activities produce pollutants, many of which pose risks to human health, the natural environment, and the Earth's biosphere. These activities, however, may have important economic and social purposes. For example, coal-fired utility plants emit a range of dangerous substances from their tall smokestacks, many of which fall back to Earth hundreds of miles downwind. These pollutants make breathing difficult for people who have asthma and heart disease, and they damage forests, lakes, rivers, and the ecosystems of which they are a part. Yet, the electrical power generated at these plants is used to run factories, provide heat and air conditioning for office buildings, light homes, and sustain the Internet.

Likewise, the internal combustion engines in automobiles and trucks emit harmful pollutants from their exhaust pipes that cause smog in urban areas and contribute to global climate change. Yet these vehicles give people the means to travel, conduct their social lives, commute to work, and move goods to markets.

These two examples illustrate the underlying contradictions, tensions, and fault lines upon which environmental politics, policy, and administration are built. Human activities that generate pollutants create benefits and impose costs. The distribution of those benefits and costs differs by areas of the country, by sectors of the economy, and among many groups and individuals within our society. For example, oil companies, automobile manufacturers, and private utility companies that own coal-fired power plants have traditionally been among the fiercest opponents of efforts to limit pollutants that degrade air quality. Environmental groups, public health groups, and elected officials in urban areas and the states of the Northeast and West Coast have been among the strongest supporters of air pollution controls.

Opponents of efforts to limit pollution generally contend that such limits lead to increased prices and lost jobs. Utility companies do incur costs when they purchase and install air pollution control equipment. Those costs are passed on to manufacturing firms, tenants in office buildings, and homeowners in the form of higher electricity bills. Yet, air pollution abatement policies reduce the number of deaths and days lost to illness among people who are vulnerable to pollutants that degrade air quality. In addition, these policies reduce damage to natural ecosystems, and they spur activities that depend on healthy ecosystems, such as swimming, boating, hiking, camping, and fishing. Various types of private, nonprofit, and public organizations that employ thousands of people support these recreational activities.

It is precisely because efforts to protect human health and the environment may lead to a redistribution of benefits and burdens within the economy and society that environmental politics, policy, and administration can be so controversial, so interesting, and so important.

In this book, we examine the efforts made by elected officials and administrators in the U.S. national government to develop and implement policies designed to limit the human and environmental damage caused by pollution.[1] Initial efforts to limit or abate pollution began in the 1950s and 1960s. The actions taken included the enactment of several public laws focused on air pollution, water pollution, and solid waste.[2] The primary objectives of these new laws included the development of research on the sources and effects of pollution, technical assistance for the states, and grants to support state and municipal pollution control activities.[3]

In 1970, a dramatic acceleration and expansion began in the national government's efforts to control the volume and types of substances that pollute the air, water, and land. In that year, President Richard Nixon and Congress took more than two dozen actions aimed at controlling pollution in order to protect human health and the environment. The four most important actions taken in 1970 are summarized below.

First, President Richard Nixon signed the National Environmental Policy Act of 1969 (NEPA) into law on January 1, 1970. The full text of the law is provided in Appendix 1. NEPA, as described by some of its framers, was designed to ensure that environmental protection and the protection of human health were included as important considerations in the U.S. government's policymaking and administrative activities. This new legislation had the overwhelming support of Congress.[4] The Senate passed the bill unanimously on December 20, 1969. The House of Representatives approved the legislation by a vote of 372 to 15 on December 22, 1969.

Second, to implement the new national policy on the environment, Congress also created, through language in NEPA, the Council on Environmental Quality (CEQ). The new agency, like the Council of Economic Advisors (CEA), was to be located in the Executive Office of the President.

Third, President Nixon, with congressional approval, created the Environmental Protection Agency (EPA). In contrast to the CEQ, however, the EPA was created through a reorganization initiative, rather than through new statutory law.[5] In submitting *Reorganization Plan No. 3 of 1970* to Congress on July 7, 1970,[6] President Nixon was acting upon a recommendation put forward in April of that year by the Ash Commission on Government Reorganization.[7] A key purpose of the president's executive branch reorganization plan, as articulated in the document itself, was to pursue a systematic approach to addressing the nation's environmental problems. President Nixon argued that the best way to achieve this goal was to establish the EPA as a new executive branch organization. It is worth noting that the CEQ strongly supported this initiative.[8]

In submitting the plan to Congress, President Nixon moved ahead of members of both the House and Senate who were working with bipartisan support on legislation to create such an agency. After Congress signaled its support for his proposed reorganization, the president acted to create the agency, and he nominated William Ruckelshaus to be its first administrator. On December 2, 1970, the Senate confirmed Ruckelshaus in that post, and the EPA officially opened for business.[9]

Fourth, Congress enacted and President Nixon signed the Clean Air Act of 1970. This legislation was designed to protect public health by reducing air pollution. The legislation also substantially strengthened the national government's authority to undertake pollution control activities. In mid-December of 1970, the members of the Senate unanimously (73–0) voted in favor of the legislation. The measure was approved in the House of Representatives by a vote of 378 to 1. On December 31, President Nixon signed the Clean Air Act of 1970 into law.[10] The principal duties of implementing this new law fell to the newly created EPA.

A NEW APPROACH TO STUDYING THE CEQ AND THE EPA

In addition to tracing the broad evolution of the pollution control policies developed between 1970 and 2010, we examine the life cycles of the two agencies created to implement these policies, the CEQ and the EPA. Specifically, we describe and attempt to explain what has happened to the CEQ and the EPA over the forty years between 1970 and 2010.[11] Thus, our study encompasses a more extended historical range than has been used in previous studies.

Another important feature of the research presented in this book is that we use a theoretical framework for our study that, to our knowledge, has not been used by other authors in published studies of the CEQ and the EPA.[12] Specifically, we employ four life cycle models—the biological, partisan political, incremental, and issue-attention models—to develop predictions about the expected paths, or trajectories, of the CEQ and the EPA between 1970 and 2010,[13] and we use budgetary resources as the basis for mapping those trajectories.

For example, the core presumption of the biological model is that factors external to the organization, especially the relative strength of the interest groups that support an agency's social mission, will be key to its budgetary resources. In contrast, the president's party and ideology, as well as the ideology of the political party that controls Congress, are presumed to be the primary factors that determine an agency's funding level in the partisan political model.

The core tenet of the incremental model is that executive branch agencies are largely buffered from "external" forces. Thus, resource levels will be relatively stable over time. In the issue-attention model, an agency's resource allocations are presumed to depend on the visibility of the issue or social problem the agency was created to "solve." As issue visibility rises, resources go up; as issue visibility goes down, resources decline.

Other unique elements of this book include the fact that we compare the actual trajectories of the CEQ and the EPA to the predicted paths, and we attempt to explain some of the differences we discovered between the predicted and actual paths of the agencies. We also compare the actual life cycle path of the CEQ to the actual path of the EPA. Then, we use the four life cycle models as a means for explaining some of the similarities among and differences between the actual life cycle paths of the two agencies.

Additionally, we use the empirical findings from our study of the CEQ and the EPA to assess the strengths and limitations of life cycle models themselves. We also systematically compare the four models by using a new analytic framework we developed for this purpose.

Finally, we use the findings of our research as a basis for offering some forecasts of the prospective paths along which environmental politics, policy, and administration in the United States may evolve over the next two decades under several political and economic scenarios.

DEFINITIONS

We offer basic definitions of three key terms used throughout this book: politics, policy, and administration. We define politics as conflict and cooperation over the distribution of benefits and burdens in society. In the United States, "politics" is often associated with competition between the Democratic and Republican parties. Indeed, conflict between members of the two parties is often referred to as "partisan politics." Conflict can also occur, however, within the Democratic and Republican parties, and, at least on some occasions, cooperation does occur in Congress across party lines.

We define public policy as public law. Our primary focus in this book is on statutory law, but administrative rules developed by agencies and "case law" that results from judicial decisions also constitute important forms of public law. Case law may consist of court interpretations of legislative intent; it may also consist of decisions about whether proper procedures were followed in the development of administrative rules.

We define public administration as the implementation of public law. The executive branch departments and agencies of the U.S. government do not have the luxury of choosing which laws they are going to implement. The assignment of implementation duties is usually found in statutory law, but executive orders, reorganization initiatives, and case law may also serve as the means by which an agency's tasks are assigned.

In sum, politics, policymaking, and administration can be intertwined. For example, attempts to pass or amend statutory law often involve bitter contests between political parties and interest groups. Likewise, the implementation of statutory law, and particularly law that involves economic and environmental regulation, generally requires the development of administrative rules. Conflict over those rules may occur, as winners in the legislative process try to preserve the benefits they have won, while losers try to minimize their losses. In short, the process of implementing public laws can be a highly charged a "political" process.

CEQ AND EPA: SIMILARITIES AND DIFFERENCES

In focusing our study of environmental politics, policy, and administration on the CEQ and the EPA, we examine two executive branch organizations that are assigned important duties in statutory law. The two organizations have a shared social or policy purpose: the protection of human health and the environment. Yet, the agencies differ significantly along several dimensions, including their location within the executive branch, primary functions, size, and complexity.

Congress designed the CEQ to be a small organization, within the Executive Office of the President, where it remains today. The Executive Office of the President, the Cabinet Departments, and the other "Independent Establishments and Government Corporations" within the Executive Branch are shown in Figure 1.1. A summary description of all parts of Figure 1.1 is provided in Appendix 2.

The presumption articulated in NEPA was that the CEQ would consist of a few dozen staff members and a budget authorization that would begin at a few hundred thousand dollars in 1971 and reach approximately one million dollars in 1973.

In creating the CEQ, the congressional authors of NEPA used the CEA as a model. The CEA was established in the Employment Act of 1946.[14] The primary task of the CEQ, like that of the CEA, is to provide direct support to the president in research, analysis, and policy recommendations. Just as the CEA prepares an annual report on the state of the economy, NEPA requires the CEQ to prepare an annual report on the condition of the environment. The CEA makes recommendations for actions that would improve economic activity, and the CEQ makes recommendations for new environmental legislation. The CEA's responsibilities include efforts to coordinate economic policy–related activities across the executive branch; the CEQ has responsibility for coordinating environmental policy implementation across the executive branch.

In contrast to the CEQ, the EPA was created with the presumption that it would be a large, independent executive branch agency. As part of President Nixon's reorganization initiative in which the EPA was created, the pollution control functions of and personnel from the Department of Health, Education, and Welfare and four other executive branch organizations were brought together into the new environmental protection agency. Thus, when it opened for business in December of 1971, the EPA

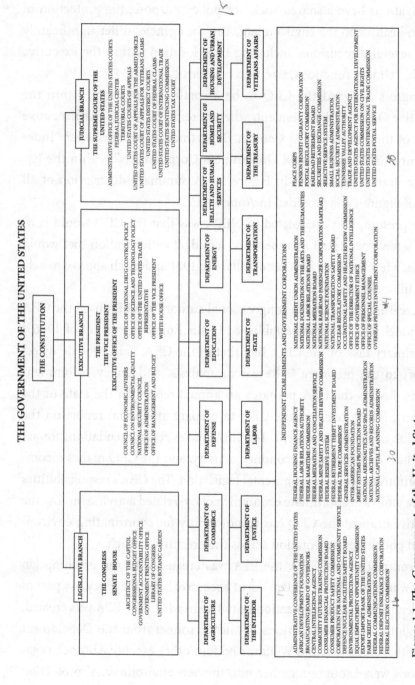

Figure 1.1 The Government of the United States.

SOURCE: The United States Government Manual 2013 November Edition (http://www.gpo.gov/fdsys/browse/collection.action?collectionCode=GOVMAN).

had almost 6,000 federal employees and budget authority of almost $1.4 billion.[15]

Additional information about the EPA's creation and its location within the Executive Branch is provided in Appendix 2.

While research was to be part of the EPA's responsibilities, the agency's primary task was to implement regulatory statutes passed by Congress. In most cases, the first step in the process of carrying out these laws involved defining, through the administrative rule-making process, the standards and practices to be applied in abating pollutants. Then, as appropriate and allowed by law, the agency was to delegate authority and resources to the states to implement the pollution control programs.

For example, under the Clean Air Act of 1970, the EPA was assigned the task of establishing and managing the regulatory control of or permitting systems for airborne pollutants. Then, as Congress passed additional environmental legislation during the 1970s, the EPA was assigned the responsibility for developing new standards and practices for pollution that affected surface water, groundwater, coastal zones, and land. To carry out these complex, large-scale functions, the EPA needed a substantial funding base and large numbers of employees and managers. The EPA also needed effective partners, in the form of fifty state environmental protection agencies, in order to do the work.

Along with highlighting the important differences between the CEQ and the EPA, it is worth noting that in some important areas the work of the two executive branch organizations has overlapped and continues to overlap. For example, in the National Environmental Policy Act of 1969, the CEQ was given the primary responsibility for developing the process by which U.S. government agencies would develop their environmental impact statements (EISs).[16] The CEQ was also assigned the authority and responsibility for conducting the reviews of those statements. Then, in large part because Senator Edmund Muskie of Maine was concerned that the EIS review process was too large a task for the CEQ, the EPA was also given responsibility, in the Clean Air Act of 1970, for reviewing EISs.[17] Ultimately, in a 1977 reorganization of the Executive Office of the President, Jimmy Carter assigned the primary responsibility for reviewing EISs to the EPA.[18] The responsibility for developing the rules governing the development of EISs, however, remained with the CEQ.

METHODOLOGY

Our examination of what happened to the CEQ and the EPA from 1970 to the present involves several steps. First, we use organizational life cycle models to predict how executive branch organizations like the CEQ and the EPA might be expected to evolve over time, particularly in terms of their organizational capacity and vitality in taking on their statutory tasks. Second, we document the actual trajectories along which these two agencies traveled between 1970 and 2010. We use changes in budgetary and staffing resources over time as key indicators of capacity and vitality. We also examine the role that leadership plays in the agencies' life histories. As scholar James Q. Wilson points out, leadership is often a key factor in whether government agencies are able to secure the external support and resources they need to function effectively.[19]

Third, we attempt to explain the reasons for the observed trajectories. We employ both qualitative and quantitative methods in collecting and analyzing data as we look for correlations between the agencies' fortunes over time and various social, political, and economic variables. Fourth, we examine the gaps between the predicted and observed trajectories of the CEQ and the EPA. We end the first part of our study by offering some conclusions about the utility of the theoretical agency life cycle models given our findings.

After completing our empirical examination of the life cycles of the CEQ and EPA over the past forty years, we attempt to predict the paths along which these two agencies—and thus U.S. environmental politics and policy more broadly—may travel over the next twenty years. While acknowledging the speculative nature of this "thought experiment" (as physicist Niels Bohr is quoted as saying, "prediction is very difficult, especially about the future"),[20] we offer forecasts based on three alternative scenarios characterized by differing but plausible social, political, and economic conditions.

ORGANIZATION OF THE BOOK

In the next chapter we review the history of environmental politics and policy in the United States from 1970 to the present. We describe the wave of major environmental laws enacted in the 1970s and the emergence of a more contentious political and policy environment in the 1980s, 1990s, and 2000s. We also consider arguments made about the strengths and weaknesses of various environmental policy tools and briefly review successes and failures in the nation's forty-year effort to reduce pollution, mitigate environmental degradation, and protect human health.

In Chapter 3, we outline the principal organizational life cycle models we use to frame our study of the CEQ and the EPA. The models are the biological model, the partisan political model, the incremental model, and the issue-attention model. In our discussion of these models, we focus on four types of variables—organizational, social, economic, and political—that might affect the budgetary resources, and thus the health, energy, and vitality, of the CEQ and the EPA.

In Chapter 4, we focus on the CEQ. We use the life cycle models to predict trajectories for the CEQ over the past forty years, taking into account the duties assigned to the CEQ and its budgetary appropriations. Then, we examine in detail the actual history of the CEQ over that time period.

In Chapter 5, we shift our focus to the EPA. We use the life cycle models as a means for making predictions about the path along which we might expect to see the EPA travel over time. Then, as with the CEQ, we examine the actual trajectory of the EPA over the past forty years.

In Chapter 6, we compare and contrast the findings we reported in Chapters 3 and 4 about the life cycles of the CEQ and the EPA. We also assess the strengths and weaknesses of the organizational life cycle models on the basis of those findings.

In Chapter 7, we look to the future. We use the findings reported in previous chapters as a baseline for predicting possible paths along which the CEQ and the EPA—and environmental politics, policy, and administration more broadly—may travel over the next twenty years in the United States under various social, political, and economic scenarios.

We conclude the book with a postscript, in which we move outside of the theoretical framework we used in the book. We do so in order to offer some additional reflections about the potential future of environmental policy and administration. We use the concept or goal of "sustainability" as the basis for organizing these reflections, and we use climate change as an example.

The National Environmental Policy Act of 1969, the Rise of Environmental Protection in the 1970s, and the Political Drama of the Next Three Decades

The National Environmental Policy Act (NEPA) was approved unanimously in the Senate and with near unanimity in the House of Representatives in December 1969. President Nixon signed the act into law on January 1, 1970. The new statute was both brief and farsighted.[1] In fewer than 3,500 words the congressional authors of NEPA articulated for the first time a national policy on the environment, set in motion an innovative regulatory process centered on environmental impact statements, institutionalized public participation in federal environmental decision making, and introduced the requirement that the president report annually to Congress on the nation's environmental status and trends.

NEPA also included a provision that established a new agency, the Council on Environmental Quality (CEQ), in the Executive Office of the President.[2] The CEQ's assigned statutory role was to implement the environmental impact statement process, prepare the president's annual environmental report on the condition of the environment, develop policy proposals for solving environmental problems, and coordinate efforts across the federal government to address environmental concerns.

As stated in the law, NEPA is designed to "encourage productive and enjoyable harmony between man and his environment"; to "promote efforts which will prevent or eliminate damage to the environment and biosphere and stimulate the health and welfare of man"; and to "fulfill the responsibilities of each generation as trustee of the environment for succeeding generations."[3]

The references to promoting harmony between people and the environment, protecting the biosphere, and affirming the nation's responsibility for environmental stewardship illustrate an understanding of the scope, scale, and significance of environmental matters that was significantly ahead of its time. The language in NEPA quoted above anticipated by twenty years the concern for the Earth's biosphere and the concept of environmental sustainability that would become more widely articulated in the run-up to the 1992 Earth Summit in Rio de Janeiro.[4] Moreover, NEPA has had an enduring global impact. By the law's fortieth anniversary, a majority of U.S. states had established their own environmental impact statement requirements and more than 160 nations worldwide had adopted similar legislation.[5]

FACTORS CONTRIBUTING TO THE CREATION OF NEPA

What led Congress to create a national policy on the environment more than forty years ago? As the CEQ noted in its first annual report, "No one can say for sure just how or why the environment burst into national prominence in 1970."[6] The report's authors, however, identified several factors that may have contributed, including the writings and actions of early environmentalists such as Henry David Thoreau, John Muir, Gifford Pinchot, and Aldo Leopold.

A related factor was the legislation enacted during the previous one hundred years that was designed to conserve natural resources, preserve wildlife, and protect natural areas. For example, Yellowstone National Park was established in 1872 and Yosemite National Park in 1890.[7] John Muir, who was a powerful voice for the preservation of natural "treasures," played a central role in the creation of Yosemite. In the early 1900s, President Theodore Roosevelt undertook a series of widely publicized efforts to create a network of national parks managed by the Department of the Interior and national forests managed by the Department of Agriculture. President Roosevelt appointed Gifford Pinchot, an active conservationist, as the first chief of the U.S. Forest Service in 1905. In sum, the establishment of national parks and national forests earned general public support in the decades before NEPA was signed into law, and the advocacy of emerging environmental nonprofit organizations, including John Muir's Sierra Club, encouraged public awareness of the need to protect the natural environment.

Major structural social and economic changes in the United States in the decades after the Second World War may also have contributed to a gradual rise in public concern for the environment. Some scholars contend that patterns can be identified in which poorer societies tend to accept substantial environmental degradation as the price of economic development. Then, as wealth increases, people begin to chafe at living with egregious pollution and manifest a willingness to pay for improved conditions. The emerging public demand for constraints on pollution in turn tends to generate political impetus for environmental regulation.[8] By the 1960s, it appears that public opinion in the United States had begun to pass through this transition in attitudes.

Historians also point to other more immediate factors that moved environmental concerns higher on the congressional policy agenda in the late 1960s and strengthened the political will for action. Rachel Carson's *Silent Spring*, published in 1962, focused public attention on the adverse effects of pervasive industrial chemicals on human health, wildlife, and the natural environment.[9]

Images of Earth taken by the Apollo 8 astronauts, the first human beings to leave the Earth's orbit and to go to the moon, also had a powerful impact. In particular, the Christmas 1968 photograph known as "Earthrise" captured the public's imagination and galvanized the environmental movement and scientific examination of the Earth. [10]

The photograph shows a small, distant planet (Earth) rising over the moon's horizon and surrounded by the deep blackness of space. The picture (Fig. 2.1) revealed Earth to be a beautiful and fragile "spaceship" on which we depend for our survival.[11] In a front-page commentary in *The New York Times* on Christmas Day 1968, poet Archibald MacLeish wrote, "To see the Earth as it truly is, small and blue and beautiful in that eternal silence where it floats, is to see ourselves as riders on the Earth together, brothers on that bright loveliness in the eternal cold—brothers who know now they are truly brothers."[12]

Two dramatic events in 1969 further heightened public concern about the environment. From January to April of that year, a major oil spill from an offshore drilling platform fouled beaches in Santa Barbara, California. Then, in June, the oily surface of the grossly polluted Cuyahoga River in Cleveland, Ohio, caught fire. Of the Santa Barbara oil spill, the editor of the Santa Barbara *News-Press* wrote: "Never in my long lifetime have I ever seen such an aroused populace at the grassroots level. This oil pollution has done something I have never seen before in Santa Barbara—it has

Figure 2.1 **"Earthrise," from Apollo 8 mission, December 1968.**
Source: NASA, http://www.nasa.gov/multimedia/imagegallery/
image_feature_1249.html.

united citizens of all political persuasions in a truly nonpartisan cause."[13] Across the United States, polling data in 1969 showed public concerns about the state of the environment at unprecedented levels.[14]

The public outcry reflected in these polling numbers added urgency to congressional deliberations. Leaders among Democratic elected officials pushing for national environmental policy legislation included Henry "Scoop" Jackson of Washington, chair of the Senate Committee on Interior and Insular Affairs and the most influential sponsor of NEPA in the Senate. One of Senator Jackson's advisors, Lynton Keith Caldwell, played a key role in writing the bill.[15] Other senior senators, particularly Edmund Muskie of Maine and Gaylord Nelson of Wisconsin, had earlier proposed similar legislation that included important ideas incorporated in the final version of the law.[16] Representative John Dingell of Michigan, chair of the House Energy and Commerce Committee, was the primary sponsor of NEPA in the House.

While Democrats held a majority in both the Senate and House in 1969 and played key leadership roles in passing this legislation, congressional action was strongly bipartisan: all Republican members of the Senate and nearly all Republicans in the House voted in favor of the bill. Furthermore, Republican elected officials, exemplified by President Theodore Roosevelt, had established a strong record over many decades as active leaders in conservation.

President Nixon initially opposed NEPA. The overwhelming bipartisan vote in favor of the bill, however, turned the president's "reluctant consent into a show of visionary statesmanship,"[17] and he signed the bill into law in a special ceremony on New Year's Day 1970. This turnabout also helped him co-opt one of the key political issues—the environment—that his potential Democratic challengers, including Scoop Jackson and Ed Muskie, were expected to emphasize in the 1972 presidential campaign.[18]

KEY ENVIRONMENTAL EVENTS AND POLICY ACTIONS OF THE 1970s

Following the signing of NEPA on January 1, 1970, several other pivotal events occurred during the remainder of that year that led the CEQ, as well as many historians and environmental policy specialists, to refer to it as "the year of the environment."[19] In April, millions of Americans participated in activities associated with the first Earth Day, a nationwide event initiated by Senator Gaylord Nelson and others. This expression of public concern and engagement fueled a competition between Congress and the president for leadership on the environment. A list of some environmental initiatives taken in 1970 by the President, Congress, and the CEQ is provided in Table 2.1.

Table 2.1. **A Sample of Executive and Legislative Branch Actions on the Environment in 1970**

Date	Action
Jan. 1	President signs NEPA
Feb. 4	President issues Executive Order 11507 on the Prevention, Control, and Abatement of Air and Water Pollution at Federal Facilities
Feb. 10	President submits a multipoint program for reducing water and air pollution
Mar. 5	President issues Executive Order 11514 on the Protection and Enhancement of Environmental Quality
Apr. 3	Congress passes Water Quality Improvement Act, Public Law 91–224
Apr. 15	President proposes legislation to end dumping of dredged spoils in the Great Lakes
May 20	President proposes treaty dealing with pollution caused by sea transportation of oil
May 23	President proposes treaty to place natural resources of the deep seabed beyond 200 miles under international regulation
June 4	CEQ publishes guidelines for environmental impact statements
June 4	President submits contingency plan for dealing with oil spills
June 11	President proposes terminating oil leases off Santa Barbara and creating a marine sanctuary
July 9	President submits to Congress a proposal to create the EPA
Aug. 3	President submits to Congress first annual report of the CEQ
Oct. 13	Congress passes Resource Recovery Act of 1970, Public Law 91–512
Dec. 2	President establishes EPA
Dec. 31	President signs Clean Air Act of 1970, Public Law 91–604

In July 1970, President Nixon proposed the creation of the Environmental Protection Agency, and in mid-December, with Senate confirmation of William Ruckelshaus as the EPA's first administrator, the agency opened for business. On December 31, 1970, with new EPA Administrator Ruckelshaus and CEQ Chair Russell Train as witnesses (Fig. 2.2), the president signed the Clean Air Act into law. This momentum continued for much of the rest of the decade as Congress enacted a wave of major environmental legislation over the next several years.

The Clean Air Act of 1970 addressed the risks of airborne pollutants at the national level. Prior to enactment of this legislation, the responsibility for air pollution control generally fell to municipal governments, with federal action limited primarily to research. The new Clean Air Act established a much more robust federal role. Under the law, the EPA set national ambient air quality standards, known as NAAQS, for six key pollutants: ozone, particulate matter, carbon monoxide, nitrogen oxides,

Figure 2.2 President Nixon signs the Clean Air Act of 1970, with William Ruckelshaus (left) and Russell Train observing.
Source: National Archives, Richard Nixon Presidential Library and Museum
Identifier: WHPO-5421-11, http://www.archives.gov/presidential-libraries/events/
centennials/nixon/photo-gallery/nixon-wh-years.html.

sulfur dioxide, and lead. The individual states were required to develop and enforce state implementation plans to achieve the standards. Regions were classified as attainment or nonattainment areas, depending on whether or not they met the NAAQS. Amendments to the law in 1977 introduced technology-based standards to limit emissions from new or significantly upgraded industrial facilities, such as power plants, factories, or other major stationary sources of air pollution. Under these standards, all firms in a given sector had to install and maintain pollution control technologies identified by the EPA as the "best available."

Thus the Clean Air Act relied primarily on the enforcement of generally applicable ambient, emissions, and technology standards to reach air quality goals. The standards-based regulatory approach, which became known as "command-and-control" or "rules-and-deterrence,"[20] has achieved substantial gains, particularly in air quality. Critics of the standards-based approach, however, contend that it lacks flexibility and is overly prescriptive, intrusive, and costly.

Legislators incorporated aspects of the standards-based model into most of the other major federal environmental statutes of the 1970s. These laws aimed to clean up the nation's surface water and groundwater (Clean Water Act of 1972), regulate pesticides (Federal Insecticide, Fungicide, and Rodenticide Act of 1972), ensure the quality of drinking water (Safe Drinking Water Act of 1974), manage the disposal of solid and hazardous waste (Resource Recovery and Conservation Act of 1976), control the use of potentially dangerous chemicals (Toxic Substances Control Act of 1976), and clean up existing hazardous waste sites (Comprehensive Environmental Response, Compensation, and Liability Act of 1980, more commonly known as Superfund). Presidents Nixon, Ford, and Carter signed these bills into law.

POLLUTION CONTROL POLICY DEVELOPMENT IN THE 1980s AND 1990s

By 1980, other domestic and international issues, such as a problematic economy and American hostages in Iran, had come to dominate the national agenda, and enthusiasm for new environmental legislation had waned. Ronald Reagan's election as president in November 1980 on an antiregulatory platform revealed the extent to which the broad political consensus of the 1970s favoring federal action on the environment had dissipated.

The environmental laws of the 1980s were more modest in scope and objectives than those of the previous decade. In 1986 Congress passed and President Reagan signed the Emergency Planning and Community Right-to-Know Act and the Superfund Amendments and Reauthorization Act. These laws were in part a response to the December 1984 disaster in Bhopal, India, in which chemical releases from a Union Carbide plant killed thousands of local residents and injured tens of thousands more. The community right-to-know law mandated that local officials and the general public have access to information about potentially hazardous chemicals in their area. The Superfund amendments provided additional federal funds, enforcement authority, and incentives for cleaning up existing hazardous waste sites.

The next major piece of environmental legislation was the Clean Air Act Amendments of 1990, signed by President George H.W. Bush. The components of this law tell a story about the direction of U.S. environmental policy from that time forward. On the one hand, the law maintained the tradition of command-and-control regulation by continuing and even strengthening strict technology standards. On the other hand, the legislation included a large-scale application of more flexible, "market-based" or "incentive-based" regulatory approaches designed to achieve emissions targets more efficiently—that is, at lower social cost. In principle, these new policy tools should provide a means to avoid some of the inefficiencies of the one-size-fits-all mandates and, at the same time, reduce the adversarial tensions that tend to arise between the EPA and regulated industries under standards-based regimes. We discuss the movement to improve the efficiency of regulations in more detail in Chapter 7 when considering the future of U.S. environmental policy, but we offer a brief introduction here.

The market-based approach first introduced on a large scale in the 1990 Clean Air Act Amendments was a scheme of tradable permits for pollution, known as "cap-and-trade." The specific goal of this new policy initiative was to reduce the emissions of precursors of acid rain, particularly sulfur dioxide. Acid rain, which adversely affects public health and the environment in the heavily populated areas of the Northeast and Mid-Atlantic regions of the United States, had become a significant political issue in the late 1980s.

Under this policy, regulators distributed a limited number of emissions permits to the coal-fired power plants in the Ohio Valley area that were the primary sources of sulfur pollution affecting the eastern United States. Regulators aimed to achieve the overall emissions reduction target by limiting the number of permits, known as allowances, to below business-as-usual levels. Under a cap-and-trade system, the total permitted amount of pollution, set by the number of allowances distributed, is known as the "cap." Since by design the allowances were in short supply compared to previous emissions levels, each firm had to either reduce its emissions or buy extra permits from other firms.

Companies able to reduce emissions relatively easily had incentives to do so, as they could then sell their extra permits in a market established for the purpose. This buying and selling of permits is the "trade" component of the cap-and-trade policy. In principle under such a system the total social cost of achieving pollution reduction goals will be lower than under a mandated technology standard because firms that can reduce emissions more cheaply will do most of the cleanup and be compensated by the other firms that buy their extra permits.

In practice, this novel approach was highly successful, garnering praise from both industry and environmental advocates. It reduced sulfur pollution and did so more cheaply than even the program's developers had anticipated. Following the success of tradable permits for sulfur emissions, policymakers and environmental advocates began to look for ways to use cap-and-trade and other variations of incentive-based policies to address a range of problems related to pollution and overexploitation of natural resources. For example, the Kyoto Protocol international agreement of 1997, designed to address the carbon emissions that contribute to climate change, included many market-based components, largely as a result of strong lobbying by U.S. negotiators who wanted to build on the successful American experience with controlling sulfur emissions.

European nations generally resisted the American emphasis on market approaches in the Kyoto negotiations of 1997. Within a few years, however, the roles had reversed: the European Union adopted the market concept and implemented a cap-and-trade program for carbon emissions among its member nations, while the United States refused to ratify the Kyoto Protocol, primarily on the grounds that the harm to the nation's economy would be too high and that major developing countries, particularly China and India, were not required to contribute to global reductions.

POLLUTION CONTROL POLICY IN THE TWENTY-FIRST CENTURY

The pattern of enthusiasm for and then rejection of market-based pollution control programs continued in American politics during the first decade of the twenty-first century. In the 2008 presidential election campaign, for example, both Republican John McCain and Democrat Barack Obama endorsed a cap-and-trade program for carbon emissions in the United States. After the election, however, a major energy policy bill that included such a program failed in Congress in 2010. Since fossil fuel combustion is a primary source of carbon emissions, the energy industry has been a consistent opponent of limits to this type of pollution. In the debate over the energy bill in 2010, industry lobbying that highlighted short-term direct costs of cap-and-trade ultimately prevailed over those arguing that long-term social benefits would outweigh short-term economic burdens.

A BRIEF REVIEW OF ENVIRONMENTAL OUTCOMES

What is the track record of the environmental policy activism of the 1970s? How much better off are human health and the environment today than they would have been without the major legislation enacted in that decade? These are complex questions. It is often hard to separate the direct effects of particular laws from the indirect effects of other changes, such as new technologies, shifting consumer demands, heightened international competition, and the restructuring of the economy toward the service sector and away from manufacturing.

Nevertheless, it is possible to identify some successes and failures. On the negative side, although American rivers rarely catch fire any more, overall gains in surface water and groundwater quality are disappointing. Many of the U.S. surface waters remain untested for quality.[21] Authorities continue to post advisories against eating fish caught in many Eastern rivers. The Chesapeake Bay has at best stable or slightly improving indicators despite several decades of effort and the expenditure of billions of dollars.[22] The great aquifers of the West and Midwest are being depleted at unsustainable rates.[23] Hydraulic fracturing—more commonly known as fracking—brings new energy sources to market but also carries with it risks of groundwater contamination.[24]

The problem of hazardous and toxic chemicals is also unresolved. While some hazardous waste sites have been cleaned up, often at enormous cost, many others continue to need attention.[25] The EPA lacks the mandate or resources to test the majority of the thousands of chemicals on the market. The nation has yet to determine where and how it will store radioactive waste for the long term.

The adverse human health effects of these less-than-ideal outcomes are relatively modest, however, compared to what would have happened if air pollution had continued unchecked at earlier levels. Almost all Americans have clean drinking water and are isolated from dangerous exposure to the worst hazardous wastes. Yet we all breathe the air and most of us live in metropolitan areas, which tend to have a higher risk of harmful air pollution. Thus, it is positive news that the strongest environmental progress over the past forty years has come in air quality.[26] Moreover, these gains have occurred despite substantial growth in population and per capita income, which would otherwise be expected to generate increased pollution.

As mentioned earlier, the Clean Air Act of 1970 identified six air pollutants that deserved special attention: ozone, particulate matter, carbon monoxide, nitrogen oxides, sulfur dioxide, and lead. These pollutants cause a range of human health problems, from respiratory and cardiac ailments to neurological damage.[27] Concentrations in the air beyond natural background levels result primarily from the combustion of fossil fuels, for example the coal used in power plants and the gasoline used in motor vehicles, and from other industrial activities. In this section we briefly document the trends for these pollutants over the past thirty years.[28]

Overall the outcomes reveal marked improvements. While from 1980 to 2012 U.S. annual gross domestic product, a measure of the nation's economic activity, more than doubled (up 133 percent), combined annual emissions for the six pollutants dropped by two-thirds (down 67 percent). The EPA reports reductions for all six pollutants, although trends vary among them.

The following list presents trends since 1980 for lead, carbon monoxide, sulfur dioxide, nitrogen oxides, and ozone as reported by the EPA:

- Lead emissions have declined by 99 percent, and lead pollution in ambient air at monitored sites has dropped by an average of 91 percent. These gains—achieved primarily by eliminating the use of lead as an additive in gasoline—are particularly important because lead causes neurological damage, especially in children.
- Carbon monoxide emissions have declined by 72 percent, and ambient air pollution at monitored sites has dropped by 83 percent.
- Sulfur dioxide emissions have declined by 79 percent, and ambient air pollution at monitored sites has dropped by 78 percent. Part of these gains followed implementation of the cap-and-trade program for sulfur dioxide required by the Clean Air Act Amendments of 1990.
- Nitrogen oxide emissions in general have dropped by 59 percent, and ambient air pollution for nitrogen dioxide in particular at monitored sites has dropped by 60 percent.
- Ozone ambient air pollution levels have declined by a more modest 25 percent. This pollutant remains a persistent problem, particularly in heavily populated metropolitan areas during hot

summer weather when the air is stagnant. There are no data for ozone emissions because this pollutant is not emitted directly. Rather, it forms as other precursor chemicals react in the air in the presence of sunshine.

Trends for particulate matter are a little more complicated to present. Under the Clean Air Act of 1970, the EPA initially established NAAQS for what were characterized as total suspended particulates. In 1987, the agency changed its focus to particulate matter under 10 micrometers in diameter, known as PM10. These particles are small enough to evade the body's natural defenses in the airway at the nose and mouth and to make their way to the lungs, where they cause harm. Following the emergence of evidence that smaller particles (less than 2.5 micrometers in diameter) can be more dangerous, the EPA added an ambient air quality standard for PM2.5 in 1997.[29] The EPA reports that ambient air pollution of PM10 at monitored sites has dropped by 39 percent since 1990 and that PM2.5 pollution, measured by equivalent techniques, has dropped by 37 percent since 2000.

Thus, efforts to mitigate air pollution under the Clean Air Act have made substantial progress. Most areas of the country are in compliance with air quality standards for most pollutants, even though the standards have been toughened over time. Of the six key pollutants identified in the 1970 law, ozone and PM2.5 remain the most troublesome. The EPA reports for 2012 that under adverse weather conditions 133.2 million people still live in nonattainment areas for ozone and 28.2 million live in nonattainment areas for PM2.5.[30]

The Clean Air Act requires the EPA to set air quality standards that protect human health with an adequate margin of safety for even the most vulnerable in society without regard to cost. Nevertheless, executive orders in place since the Reagan administration require federal agencies to conduct analyses showing that the social benefits of regulations are likely to exceed the social costs. Both the EPA and independent analysts have attempted to assess the costs and benefits of various components of the nation's air quality efforts.

The EPA's retrospective analysis of the overall costs and benefits of Clean Air Act regulation from 1970 to 1990, for example, estimated that benefits outweighed costs by a factor of between ten and a hundred to one.[31] Independent analysts, while skeptical of the EPA's high benefit–cost ratios, still generally agree that benefits have outweighed costs by a significant margin.[32] A study of the impact of Clean Air Act regulations since 1990 found that the benefits of regulations reducing emissions of sulfur dioxide, nitrogen oxides, and PM2.5 have benefit–cost ratios on the order of forty to one.[33]

When the EPA periodically proposes new, stricter regulations for ozone and PM2.5, competing—often politically motivated—prospective analyses quickly appear indicating that the new regulations would not pass the cost–benefit test or would pass the test easily even if set at more stringent levels. However, retrospective tests by independent analysts generally show that the nation's air quality regulations that began in 1970 have been a good public investment.

SUMMARY

During the 1970s, Democrats and Republicans in Congress worked together to pass a series of major environmental acts. These bipartisan actions were taken in response to the many visible environmental problems the country faced and the adverse health effects caused by pollutants that were being put into the air, land, surface water, and groundwater. By the end of the 1970s, the political will for action had weakened and an antiregulatory backlash had emerged. Ronald Reagan's election in 1980 signaled the end of consistent bipartisan support for environmental regulation. Despite occasional periods of reduced partisanship allowing for some progress, such as passage of the 1990 Clean Air Amendments, federal action on the environment has been bogged down in partisan gridlock. All the major laws of the 1970s need updating to take into account changed environmental conditions, advances in scientific knowledge, and improvements in our understanding of policy efficiency and effectiveness. However, the current political stalemate makes this impossible in the near term.

Life Cycle Models of Organizations

The executive branch departments and agencies of the national government have the key role in the implementation stage of the policy process. In the National Environmental Policy Act of 1969 (NEPA), the Council on Environmental Quality (CEQ) was assigned the task of providing an annual report on the condition of the nation's environment, assessing the effects of national, state, and local governments' efforts to protect the environment, and developing recommendations to improve environmental quality. The Environmental Protection Agency (EPA) was given the primary responsibility for implementing the pollution control laws Congress created between 1970 and 1980, amendments to those laws, and new laws enacted during the next three decades.

Some scholars have maintained that the process of implementing a public law is "removed from the hurry and strife of politics," since the important political and substantive matters have been decided in the law itself.[1] Other scholars, however, describe the implementation stage of the policy process as a continuation of the political struggle that occurred over the creation of the law.[2]

The competition between these two views of policy implementation is one factor that makes the study of the "life cycles" of executive branch departments and agencies so important. If the first view is correct, the implementation of a public law should be a relatively smooth process in which the leadership, managers, and professionals in agencies like the CEQ and the EPA carry out their assigned statutory duties. Likewise, the life cycle of the executive branch agency should be relatively stable and long. Finally, absent serious flaws in the design of the policy itself, the prospects for successful implementation of the law might seem to be relatively high.

If the alternative view of policy implementation is correct, however, the extent to which implementation of a public law actually occurs is likely to depend heavily on the health, vitality, and even survival of the implementing agency. In turn, the health and vitality of the executive branch agency is likely to depend on the leadership of the agency and the resources that Congress and the president appropriate for it.

In this chapter, we outline and provide background on the four agency life cycle models we use to frame our research on the CEQ and the EPA: (1) the biological model, (2) the partisan political model, (3) the incremental model, and (4) the issue-attention model. Among the reasons we chose these four models is because the scholars who developed them and employ them in the academic literature focus on different variables that affect the resources, health, vitality, and survival of an executive branch organization. For example, some scholars focus on the leadership and assigned task of the agency; some focus on the elected officials and interest groups; others focus on the press, dramatic events or crises, and public opinion. It is also worth noting that competing views of what constitutes the key variables in determining agency appropriations can also be found in the broader literature on national government appropriations and policy decision making.[3]

Within the academic literature, the variables that are presumed to affect an agency's resources, health, and vitality have typically been divided into

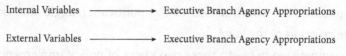

Figure 3.1 Key Variables that Determine Agency Appropriation.

two types: internal and external.[4] A simple schematic diagram of the two types of causal variables and their presumed effects on agency appropriations is presented in Figure 3.1.

The information in Figure 3.1 provides a useful conceptual starting point for an examination of the biological, partisan political, incremental, and issue-attention models. The next step we will take in presenting the four models is to provide a list of the key internal variables and external variables scholars generally associate with each model. These variables are presented in Table 3.1. In the table, the variables considered to be the primary independent variables in each of the four models are highlighted in bold print.

As shown in Table 3.1, the internal variables in the biological model include the executive branch agency's social function or purpose, leadership, professional staff, performance, age, and size. Each of these factors could have an effect on the agency's resources, but the presumption in the biological model is that external variables will have the biggest effect on an agency's resources. The external variables include Congress, interest groups, functional rivals, and allocational rivals.

In the partisan political model, the internal variables include the agency's social function and its leadership. The external variables include the president, Congress, functional rivals, and allocational rivals. The presumption in this model is that external variables will be the key factor in shaping or determining the agency's resources.

The "internal" variables in the incremental model are the executive-branch agency, the Office of Management and Budget (OMB), the appropriations committees in the House and Senate, and the interest groups that benefit from the agency's programs. These internal variables are considered to be the key factors that shape or determine an executive branch agency's resources.

Table 3.1. **KEY VARIABLES DETERMINING AGENCY RESOURCES IN THE FOUR LIFE CYCLE MODELS**

Model	Internal variables	External variables
Biological	Agency social function	**Congress**
	Agency leadership	**Interest groups**
	Agency professional staff	**Functional rivals**
	Agency performance	**Allocational rivals**
	Agency age	
	Agency size	
Partisan political	Agency social function	**President** (party/ideology)
	Agency leadership	**Congress** (party majority/ ideology)
		Elections
Incremental	**Agency**	Economy (growth, decline)
	Office of Mgt. & Budget	Party control of Congress
	Appropriations committees	Expenditure targets/limits
	Interest groups	Overall level of domestic spending
Issue-attention	Agency social function	**Social problems**
		Events/crises
		Media coverage
		Public opinion
		Congress
		Distribution of costs/ benefits

Bold print signifies primary independent variables in each model.

In the issue-attention model, the agency's social function is considered the key internal variable. The external variables include social problems, events or crises that highlight the significance or severity of these social problems, media coverage of these events or crises, public opinion about these social problems, Congress, and the ways in which benefits and burdens associated with these social problems and attempts to respond to them are distributed. The presumption in this model is that external models will be the key to whether an executive branch agency's resources grow or shrink.

Among the key patterns that can be identified by comparing and contrasting the list of key variables in the four models is that external variables are the key causal factors in three of those models. The incremental model is the only model in which internal variables are considered to be the key causal factor in determining an agency's appropriations. Yet, three of the four "internal" variables in the incremental model exist outside the executive branch agency. Thus, these variables would be considered "external" variables in the biological, partisan political, and issue-attention models.

Why are the OMB, congressional appropriations committees, and interest groups considered to be "internal" variables in the incremental model? The key presumption of scholars who use the incremental model to describe, explain, and make predictions about appropriations is this: decisions about an executive branch agency's appropriations are buffered or protected from "external" forces by the (relatively) "closed" negotiations among the agency, the OMB, the congressional appropriations committees, and the interest groups that support or benefit from the agency's programs.[5]

As indicated in Table 3.1, however, some scholars who have employed the incremental model in studies of U.S. government budgeting have identified "external" variables that they believe can be used to enhance the predictive and explanatory power of the incremental model.[6] Other scholars who contend that the incremental model is the best or most useful tool for explaining and predicting agency appropriations, however, do not consider external variables to be important causal factors.[7]

As a means of summing up the key findings reported above, schematic diagrams of the linkages between the primary causal variables and agency appropriations are presented in Figure 3.2 for each of the four life cycle models.

In the remainder of the chapter, we will provide a still more complete description of each model. Specifically, we will identify the founding

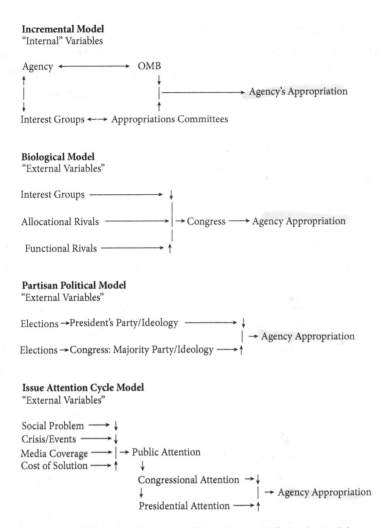

Figure 3.2 Schematic Diagrams of Four Agency Life Cycle Models.

scholar or scholars of each model, and we will summarize some of the relevant scholarly literature that has developed in relationship to each model. At the end of each of these four descriptive sections, we will use the models as tools for developing predictions about the expected life cycle trajectories of the CEQ and the EPA between 1970 and 2010. These predictions will be compared to the actual life cycle paths of the two organizations in Chapters 4 and 5.

We begin the discussion of the four agency life cycle models with the biological model, in large part because the "birth" of new organizations is a key part of that model. As previously noted, our study of the life cycles of the CEQ and the EPA begin with the birth of those two organizations in 1970.

BIOLOGICAL MODEL

Although Anthony Downs was not the first scholar to use the field of biology as a basis for thinking about human organizations,[8] he did so very effectively in his 1967 book *Inside Bureaucracy*.[9] In that book, Downs took the position that human organizations, like all living organisms, are born, grow, age, and die. He argued that this life cycle applied to all organizations, regardless of their purpose, size, or sector.[10]

Downs identified several ways in which a new human organization could come into existence, but he also noted that a new bureau may not survive its infancy. Among the key factors that might contribute to an agency's survival is a founding leader who is strongly committed to the organization's assigned social functions and energetic in pursuit of support for the organization. Downs also contends, however, that new bureaus can only grow rapidly enough and continue long enough to pass the *"initial survival threshold"* (emphasis in original) if the organization's leadership secures support from politicians who control the agency's budget and from the clients who would benefit from the "social functions" or programs provided by that bureau.[11]

The support of these politicians and interest groups is essential because they protect the agency from attacks by functional and allocational rivals that exist within and outside the governmental system. For example, other executive branch organizations that have environmental protection or the protection of human health as part of their mission might be both functional and allocational rivals for the EPA within the national government. Likewise, private sector organizations, such as utility plants and chemical companies, might be functional rivals because the EPA is assigned the task of limiting the pollutants those types of private sector organizations put into the air, water, and land. Thus, we can predict that these private sector organizations are likely to resist the growth of a regulatory agency like the EPA, and we can predict that they may even mount a concerted campaign to discredit and kill the agency.

The next three stages of Downs's agency life cycle are maturity, aging, and, at least potentially, death. Downs seems to believe that the adult or mature stage of a bureau's life is likely to be relatively stable and long. An agency's leadership and the quality of its professional staff will be important factors in achieving this stability. Yet, external forces may be even more important to an agency's long-term trajectory than its leadership. In fact, Downs says that the "major causes of both growth and decline in bureaus are rooted in exogenous factors in their environment."[12]

With respect to aging, Downs says organizations, like people, change as they get older. Initially, some of the changes can be positive. Mature agencies with experienced personnel can be more efficient, producing stronger results with the same level of resources. Over the longer term, however, aging in agencies leads to stagnation and declining talent. Once an agency ceases to grow, it loses energetic climbers, and replaces them with "conservers." Likewise, as the agencies' leaders age, they become much less energetic in the pursuit of the organization's key social function.

Even though he thinks sclerosis is likely to develop in an aging agency, Downs contends that the older a bureau becomes, the less likely it is to die. Although he does not provide any data to support his position, Downs argues the "death rate" among both bureaus, as well as oligopolistic private firms, is very low. Most agencies, Downs argues, live on, either independently or as a swallowed-up unit within some other "aggrandizing bureau," until the government that created them is overthrown.

Despite the powerful argument Downs offers about the key role that exogenous factors play in the survival of an agency, and, despite his emphasis on the important role that internal variables such as leadership, professional staff, social function, and age play in an agency's survival, Downs concludes his argument about agency life cycles with a bit of a surprise. In the end, he seems to say that the size of an organization, a key internal factor, will ultimately be the pivotal variable that determines whether it lives on or dies.[13]

Downs's application of the biological life cycle model to study public, non-profit, and private organizations added an important dimension to the study of human organizations. His work also seems, at least in part, to have stimulated some new work on the subject of organizational life cycles. For example, Peter Drucker took up the topic in his 1969 book *The Age of Discontinuity*,[14] as did Herbert Kaufman in his 1972 book *The Limits of Organizational Change*.[15] Drucker's focus was primarily on private sector organizations, while Kaufman's focus was primarily on government organizations.

Then, in 1976, Herbert Kaufman published what quickly became the classic study of whether government agencies die—and when and how they are born. Kaufman's book is titled *Are Government Organizations Immortal?*[16] Taking on this task, Kaufman notes, was a formidable undertaking, since for "organizations, birth, death, and therefore longevity, are elusive concepts."[17] This situation, Kaufman notes, stands in sharp contrast to the death of a human, which is "comparatively easy to identify."[18]

In his attempt to determine whether government organizations die or live eternally, Kaufman examines the agencies in "10 of the 11 executive branch departments in existence in 1973 and the Executive Office of the President."[19] Specifically, he "compares the list of federal agencies in existence in 1923 and 1973."[20] Excluded from his examination of executive-branch departments is the Defense Department, in part because it is so massive and atypical that data from it might overwhelm the other data. The U.S. Post Office, which was a cabinet department in 1923, is also excluded for similar reasons. Finally, Kaufman excluded more than fifty "independent agencies" and "scores of special boards, commissions, and committees."[21] For these reasons and others, Kaufman is careful to define his study as an initial, exploratory step, not a comprehensive study.

Kaufman reports that of the 175 organizations in the 1923 sample, 148 of them (85 percent) were still in existence in 1973. Some of these organizations existed in very different and diminished form; many had been moved into other existing executive branch organizations or into newly created organizations. Of the twenty-seven executive branch organizations that disappeared over this time period, the age of death varied

org.
more created
btwn 23-73

substantially from the early years to mature years. Kaufman also reports that the deaths—as well as the births—of executive branch agencies tended to occur in bunches, and he reports that the births of new agencies between 1923 and 1973 substantially exceeded the deaths of existing organizations.

The Great Depression of the 1930s was one of the time periods in which many executive branch organizations were created, grew, and, in some cases, died. Among the best-known and most frequently cited studies of an executive branch agency that was born during this period of time are two books on the Tennessee Valley Authority (TVA), created in 1933. David E. Lilienthal's *TVA—Democracy on the March* appeared first,[22] followed by Philip Selznick's *TVA and the Grass Roots*.[23] The two studies offer fascinating, albeit competing, views of the TVA's birth and evolution.

Perhaps the most compelling of all of the case studies written about the birth, evolution, and death of an executive branch agency created during the Great Depression—or any other era for that matter—is Louis C. Gawthrop's study of the Resettlement Agency.[24] Franklin Roosevelt created the Resettlement Agency in 1935 by executive order to help farm families who were most severely affected by the economic and ecological catastrophe of that period.[25] Yet, according to Gawthrop, the very existence of this organization "represented an ideological challenge to the status quo," and the agency's remarkable performance generated a counter-reaction that resulted in its demise (Congressional termination).[26]

Other scholars have also chronicled the birth, the evolution, and sometimes the death of executive branch organizations with birthdates that came after the starting point for Kaufman's study. For example, in his book *Bureaucracy: What Government Agencies Do and Why They Do It*, James Q. Wilson examines the TVA, the Federal Maritime Authority, the Civil Aeronautics Board, the National Highway Safety Transportation Board, the Occupational Safety and Health Administration, and the Food and Drug Administration.[27] In these case studies, Wilson examines the way in which factors in the birth and early development of a U.S. government organization serve as a means for explaining its trajectory.

The contemporary public administration literature also includes a number of published studies on the life cycles of state executive branch organizations. For example, in a 1985 publication, James K. Conant examined the birth of the New Jersey Department of Environmental Protection in 1970, the growth of the organization, and the key factors that contributed to its birth and rapid growth. A second study by Conant, published in 1989, contained a comparative study of the life cycles of four New Jersey executive branch organizations. The growth and decline in the resources of those organizations, as well as the factors that were driving the changes in resource levels, were focal points of the study.[28]

Over the past fifteen years or so, the findings Herbert Kaufman reported in his book *Are Government Organizations Immortal?* have been critiqued and extended by a number of scholars, including Daniel P. Carpenter and David E. Lewis, working individually and in collaboration.[29] In his 2002 article "The Politics of Agency Termination: Confronting the Myth of Agency Immortality," Lewis offered findings that were in sharp contrast to those of Kaufman. Lewis concluded that government organizations have a relatively high rate of death. Specifically, he found that "more than half of all agencies created since 1946 and listed in the USGM [United States Government Manual] were terminated prior to 1997."[30]

Differences in methodology may have contributed to the differences in the findings of Kaufman and Lewis. Those differences include the sources of data employed, the time period studied, and the definition of "death" employed by the two authors.

THE PARTISAN POLITICAL MODEL

A second model that can be used to describe and explain the life cycles of public agencies is the partisan political model. There is no evident founding or dominant scholar who can be easily associated with this model. Rather, the partisan political model can be considered a natural outgrowth of the political science literature on elections and parties and, more recently, presidential transitions. In this model, the primary assumption is that majority parties in legislative institutions, and, even more importantly, newly elected presidents, will attempt to control governmental activity by trying to control the executive branch departments and agencies.

In this model, the level of support a government agency receives, its vitality, and even its survival depend on whether its social purpose or function aligns with the priorities, and perhaps even more importantly the ideology, of the political party that controls the presidency and Congress. Particularly since Ronald Reagan's election in 1980, for example, Republicans have become increasingly opposed to economic and environmental regulation, while Democrats have been more likely to support both.

Thus, in a case where the election of a new president involves a change in party, as it did in Reagan's case, we might expect to see change in a regulatory agency's fortunes. Likewise, if the election also puts the new president's party in control of both chambers of Congress, we might expect to see a significant change in a regulatory agency's fortunes. Such circumstances have been relatively rare over the past forty years, however, while divided government has been relatively common.

In cases where a president is from one party and the other party controls Congress, the effects that a pro-regulation or anti-regulation presidential agenda will have on regulatory agencies are likely to be more complex and difficult to predict. In this case, the branches of government may engage in power struggles over the prestige of and the support afforded to various agencies. If Congress favors an agency, for example, it may appropriate more funds than the president requests for the agency. Even if the president signs the appropriation bill, however, the new funding may not appear in the president's future budget recommendations.

Alternatively, if Congress declines to enact components of the White House agenda, the president may act independently by executive order or other means. These dynamics can become more complicated if control of Congress is divided, or if one or both houses have precarious majorities. Following this logic, agencies with relatively low profiles relative to contemporary controversies may not be much affected by political cycles, while the fortunes of those in the center of ongoing debates may rise or fall significantly.

Even in the case of divided government, however, the partisan political model can be especially visible during presidential transitions from one party to the other. Specifically, agencies that have statutorily assigned tasks (or social functions) of particular interest to that party or president are likely to find that a president will nominate for top leadership positions people who are sympathetic to the agency's mission. In addition, these agencies are likely to experience increased budgets and staffing. In contrast, agencies that focus on social functions devalued by the party in power may be subjected to unsympathetic or hostile political appointees and periods of budgetary and staffing starvation.

For example, in his 1981 inaugural address, President Reagan famously said: "government is not the solution to our problem; government is the problem."[31] Not surprisingly, the Reagan administration immediately began efforts to overturn, block, or delay policy development and implementation in the areas of economic, health and safety, and environmental regulation. A key element of the Reagan administration's strategy was to put into the executive branch departments and agencies political appointees whose ideological beliefs were similar to the president's and whose loyalty to the president would be unquestioned. In addition, the Reagan administration made an energetic effort to cut the budgets and staff of organizations involved in these regulatory (or "social") functions.

The political science, public administration, and environmental policy literatures contain a wide range of studies that explicitly or implicitly seem to be built upon the political model described above. Recent examples of published literature on environmental policy and regulation that provide substantial support for the partisan political model include Norman J. Vig's 2006 book chapter titled "Presidential Leadership and the Environment" and Michael E. Kraft's 2006 chapter titled "Environmental Policy in Congress."[32]

DEVELOPING PREDICTIONS ON THE BASIS OF THE BIOLOGICAL AND PARTISAN POLITICAL MODELS

Using the *biological model* to predict the life histories of the CEQ and the EPA, we would expect to see an energetic leader directing the organization and actively pursuing budgetary resources and staff in the early stages of the agency's life, at least to the point where it passes through the "initial survival threshold." Then, we would expect to see a gradual increase in agency resources over time, until bureaucratic aging begins to occur. At that point, budgetary resources and personnel might remain static or even decline somewhat. These predictions for the biological model are presented schematically in Figure 3.3.

If we use the *partisan political model* as the basis for prediction, however, we would expect to see a more variable, contingent path for the CEQ and the EPA. Specifically, we would expect to see agency leadership change as a new president comes into office, reflecting the president's ideology. With respect to appropriations and staffing levels, we might expect to see a wavelike pattern, in which presidents sympathetic to the agency's statutory social function provide increased resources and demand more vigorous activity, whereas presidents unsympathetic to the agency's core function cut budgetary resources and personnel and otherwise

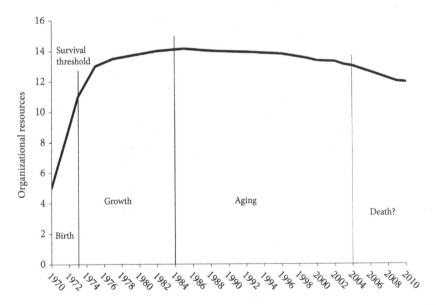

Figure 3.3 Schematic Prediction of Agency History from the Biological Model.
NOTE: The y-axis represents a generic, arbitrary scale reflecting the predicted level of resources available to the agency. The vertical reference lines provide schematic markers for the life cycle stages predicted by Downs in *Inside Bureaucracy.*

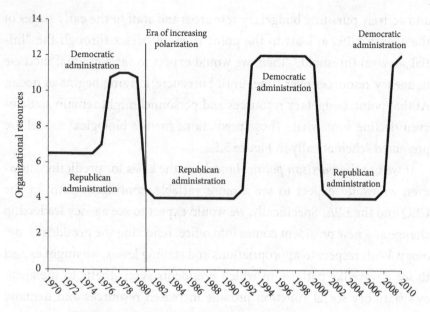

Figure 3.4 Schematic Prediction of Agency History from the Partisan Political Model.

NOTE: The y-axis represents a generic, arbitrary scale reflecting the predicted level of resources available to the agency. The vertical reference line indicates the beginning of the period of increased political polarization marked by the election of President Reagan in 1980.

hinder agency action. In short, to generalize, we would expect to see the CEQ and the EPA fare better under Democratic administrations than under Republican administrations, recognizing that the ideological split between the two major parties over the environment became substantially stronger and more clearly defined following the election of Ronald Reagan in 1980.

These predictions for the partisan political model are presented schematically in Figure 3.4.

THE INCREMENTAL MODEL

The incremental model is usually employed as a model of policy or administrative decision making, but it can also be used as an agency life cycle model. Indeed, the most important empirical testing of the incremental model has focused on changes in the budgetary resources appropriated to executive branch departments and agencies from year to year and over time.

Economist Charles E. Lindblom provided the classic articulation of the incremental model. The original version of Lindblom's analysis and argument was published in his 1959 article "The Science of 'Muddling Through.'"[33] Lindblom went on to more fully develop his argument in two books: *A Strategy of Decision*, co-authored with David Braybrooke in 1963,[34] and *The Intelligence of Democracy* in 1965.[35]

In "The Science of 'Muddling Through,'" Lindblom argues that the two principal models of decision making are the "root" or "rational-comprehensive" model, and the "branch" or incremental model. The rational-comprehensive model, Lindblom notes, is what graduate students are taught to use in academic classrooms. In governmental decision making, however, Lindblom contends that the incremental model best describes the way that elected officials and public administrators make decisions.

According to Lindblom, elected officials and administrators begin with existing policy and only consider modest adjustments to that policy. In other words, decision makers are attempting to ameliorate, rather than solve, policy or administrative problems. Thus, "good policy" is determined by what decision makers can agree upon.

In contrast, solving problems is the presumed objective in the rational-comprehensive model. Thus, decision makers begin by defining a problem and listing all of the values or goals that are to be realized in pursuit of a solution to the problem. Then, all possible approaches to solving the problem are identified. The approach that offers the best possible result for the least possible cost is selected.

Lindblom maintains that there are a variety of reasons why elected officials and administrators almost always use the incremental model, rather than the rational-comprehensive model, to make decisions. The reasons include limits of time, resources, and knowledge. The high risk of unintended consequences that almost always accompanies a large-scale change in policy is another important reason. In addition, Lindblom argues that elected officials and administrators use the incremental approach to decision making because they want to avoid conflict over basic values that a non-incremental approach could generate. Such conflict, Lindblom contends, could open up deep fissures in a democratic society that might pose a risk to its survival.

A number of scholars have made efforts to examine and test the incremental model. These efforts include both qualitative and empirical approaches, with the latter focused on government budgeting. For example, in an early empirical test of the incremental model, Davis, Dempster, and Wildavsky examined budgeting in the national government. In their 1966 publication "A Theory of the Budgeting Process,"[36] the three scholars reported that changes in department and agency budgets generally occurred at the margins. The explanation Davis, Dempster, and Wildavsky offered for this finding was that budgets were determined through negotiations among four key players: agency leadership, OMB, congressional committees, and interest groups. These four participants were identified as "internal" variables.

In a follow-up study published in 1974, the same three scholars largely confirmed their earlier findings in an article titled "Toward a Predictive Theory of Government Expenditure: US Domestic Appropriations."[37] The results were important for a number of reasons, including the fact that the authors attempted to add new environmental or external variables to their models. The findings indicated that in about one quarter of the fifty-four agencies examined, political, economic, or social variables did affect the appropriation. Yet, the authors held to their earlier conclusion that appropriations are largely determined by "internal" variables.

Despite the potential importance of their conclusions, the work of Davis, Dempster, and Wildavsky did not settle a host of important methodological questions about budgetary incrementalism. These questions include: What constitutes an incremental change? Is a 2 percent, 5 percent, 10 percent, or even 15 percent change in a base budget an incremental change? What constitutes a base budget? Is the base the agency's prior-year appropriation or prior-year expenditure, or is it a "current services" figure, which includes the estimated cost of inflation and new or expanded program requirements set in law? What is the proper level of analysis for examining budgeting? Is the departmental level, the agency or bureau level, or the program level the best level for examining budgets?

An attempt to grapple with some of these questions and extend previous budgetary research was undertaken by Auten, Bozeman, and Cline. Their work was published in a 1984 article titled "A Sequential Model of Congressional Appropriations."[38] The authors did not reject Davis, Dempster, and Wildavsky's general conclusion about the important effect internal variables had on budgetary outcomes, but they did note that "Empirical studies of agency appropriations . . . suggest that agency success is related to aggregate economic and political variables such as the unemployment rate and partisan strength in Congress."[39]

Auten, Bozeman, and Cline also took the position that "environmental influences" had only been included in incremental models "on an ad hoc basis rather than being incorporated systematically into a theoretical framework."[40] Thus, their study was designed to employ a "sequential budgetary model" in the examination of "aggregate budget decisions on appropriations, allocations of appropriations among departments, and allocations among agencies in the Agriculture and Treasury departments."[41] Based on their empirical work, the authors concluded that their model provided "a superior explanation of federal budgeting."[42] Among the key factors Auten, Bozeman, and Cline added to the standard incremental model were (1) a budget constraint established on a top-down basis, and (2) external economic and political variables.

THE ISSUE-ATTENTION MODEL

The fourth life cycle model we are using in this book is the issue-attention model. This model was introduced by Anthony Downs in a 1972 publication titled "Up and Down with Ecology--The 'Issue-Attention' Cycle."[43] Downs opens the article with the observation that a sudden and dramatic surge of interest in the quality of the environment had taken place over the previous several years. He indicates that he wants to find out whether this surge of interest in the environment is unique, or whether it is an example of what frequently happens in the American political system with respect to a broad range of social problems.

Downs takes the position that rapid buildup in public attention on environmental quality could be described and explained with his issue-attention cycle model. That model is constructed around a key observation or idea: "American public attention rarely remains sharply focused upon any one domestic issue for very long—even if it involves a continuing problem of crucial importance to society."[44] Downs further argues that a social problem suddenly "leaps into prominence, remains there a short time, and then—though still largely unresolved—gradually fades from the center of public attention."[45]

Downs identifies five stages in the issue-attention cycle: (1) the pre-problem stage, (2) alarmed discovery and euphoric enthusiasm, (3) realizing the cost of significant progress, (4) gradual decline of intense public interest, and (5) the post-problem stage. The pre-problem stage exists, Downs says, when "some highly undesirable social condition exists but has not yet captured much public attention, even though some experts or interest groups may already be alarmed by it."[46]

The "alarmed discovery and euphoric enthusiasm" stage usually begins as "a result of some dramatic series of events . . . or for some other reasons, the public suddenly becomes both aware of and alarmed about the evils of a particular problem."[47] The public will demand that America's political leaders solve the problem and do so within a short period of time. This optimism, however, is likely to be based on the assumption that most obstacles to progress do not require significant changes in the social structure.

The third stage of the cycle, "realizing the cost of significant progress," is the result of a gradual realization on the part of the public that the costs of solving the problem will be high. Those costs will include a substantial amount of money, and they will include sacrifices that will have to be made by a minority, or even a majority of the public, who benefit from existing societal arrangements.

During the fourth stage of the cycle, public interest in the issue declines as citizens absorb information about the difficulties of solving the problem and about the costs they would have to pay to solve it. The result is a loss of interest in solving the problem.

In the "post-problem" or fifth stage of the issue-attention cycle, an issue moves into a prolonged limbo, and a new social problem becomes the focus of public attention. Nevertheless, Downs says that the "new institutions, programs, and policies that may have been created to solve" the problem will continue to exist, and these "entities often have an impact on public attention even after public opinion has shifted elsewhere."[48] Furthermore, it is possible that an event or circumstance may trigger short-term public attention to the old problem. Alternatively, the old problem may become visible again because it is attached in some way to a new problem that captures public attention.

Downs argues that most major social problems will go through this five-stage issue-attention cycle because they share three specific characteristics: (1) the "majority of the population is not suffering from the problem as much as some minority (a *numerical* minority, not necessarily an *ethnic* minority)"; (2) the "sufferings caused by the problem are generated by social arrangements that provide significant benefits to a majority or a powerful minority of the population"; and (3) the problem no longer has—or never had—any "intrinsically exciting qualities,"[49] so the media stops covering the issue and the public gets bored with it.

Downs believed the intensity of public interest in the quality of the environment was (already) declining in 1972, and he believed the environmental problem was moving into the fourth state of the issue-attention cycle. Yet, Downs reports that he is uncertain about when the issue of environmental quality will move into the fifth or "post-problem" stage of the issue-attention cycle.

According to Downs, there are several characteristics or strengths of the environmental quality problem that will protect it from rapid decline. One of these characteristics is that environmental pollution, particularly air pollution, is more visible and threatening than other types of social problems. The second characteristic is that pollution poses a threat to almost everyone in society. Thus, Downs argues that politicians can safely attack pollution without fear of adverse political consequences. Finally, Downs argues that the blame for pollution can be assigned to a small group of organizations, which include the auto industry, power-generating firms, and fuel-supplying firms. Downs took the position that these organizations have the power to substantially reduce pollution if they want to do so.

We think it is particularly fitting that Downs viewed ecology as a key test of his issue-attention cycle model. Downs's examination of the issue-attention cycle for ecology seems to have covered a period of time from the mid- or late 1960s to the early 1970s. Our work in this book will provide an opportunity to examine ecology and "test" the issue-attention cycle model over a forty-year period from 1970 to 2010. As part of our research, we track public interest in (or opinion on) ecology or environmental protection.

By presenting the public opinion data in our book, we provide a means for examining whether ecology moved from the fourth stage of the issue-attention cycle, where Downs located it in 1972, into the fifth stage of that cycle soon after 1972. We will also be mindful of the special characteristics Downs attributed to ecology. Finally, we will be investigating with great interest the effects that the new institutions, programs, and policies created during the 1970s and the three decades that followed had on public attention to ecology and on the pollutants that pose a risk to the quality of the environment and human health.

An extensive body of work on issue attention, or public opinion, and its relationship to public policymaking can be found in both the survey research literature and the public policy literature. A summary of that literature is beyond the scope of this study, but we think that a 2007 book chapter by Andrew Kohut provides an especially relevant perspective on Downs's issue-attention model and the ongoing relevance of the themes Downs put forward in his 1972 article. Kohut's chapter is titled "But What Do the Polls Show."[50]

Kohut frames his chapter with a comment by a leading advisor to President Kennedy, Theodore Sorenson, who indicated that public opinion was not a central concern of elected officials in the early 1960s. Kohut argues that over the fifty years that followed Kennedy's presidency, however, the "views of ordinary Americans" have had a growing impact on public policy, with public opinion polls serving as "a megaphone for the voice of the people."[51]

Kohut goes on to say: "Polls provide leaders with capital or impoverish them in their efforts to promote policies."[52] Yet, Kohut notes that public opinion can change over time, that public officials try to shape and manipulate public opinion, and that a powerful interest group may be able to override a strong tide of public opinion. In sum, Kohut's views underscore the potential value of examining Downs's issue-attention cycle model over the forty-year period of time from 1970 to 2010, and they highlight some of the factors that can blunt or block the translation of public opinion or public demands into public policy responses to social problems.

DEVELOPING PREDICTIONS ON THE BASIS OF THE INCREMENTAL AND ISSUE-ATTENTION MODELS

Using the *incremental model* to predict the life histories of the CEQ and the EPA, we would expect to see a long-term increase in budgetary resources, with marginal increases and decreases along the way. These predictions for the incremental model are presented schematically in Figure 3.5.

Using the *issue-attention model* to predict the life histories of the two agencies, we would expect to see budgets rise rapidly in response to the sudden discovery of and public alarm about an environmental issue, followed by a drop as the high costs of fixing the problem become known, other (new) problems become the focus of attention, and public attention to environmental issues wanes. The trajectory might take the form of an upside-down U during the early stages of a new agency's life cycle. Then, we expect to see an undulating wavelike pattern, as public attention and the attention public officials give to the social function of the organization decline, are renewed, then decline again and rise again.

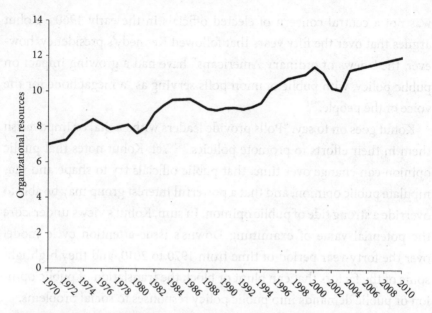

Figure 3.5 Schematic Prediction of Agency History from the Incremental Model.

NOTE: The y-axis represents a generic, arbitrary scale reflecting the predicted level of resources available to the agency.

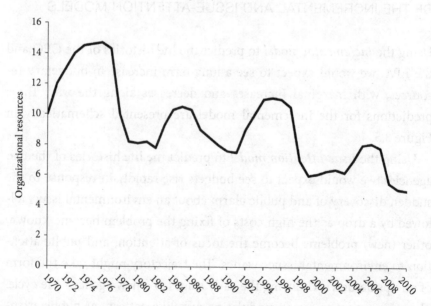

Figure 3.6 Schematic Prediction of Agency History from the Issue-Attention Model.

NOTE: The y-axis represents a generic, arbitrary scale reflecting the predicted level of resources available to the agency.

These predictions for the issue-attention model are presented schematically in Figure 3.6.

In Chapters 4 and 5, we compare the predicted paths of the CEQ and the EPA we have developed from the four agency life cycle models to the actual paths of those organizations.

The Council on Environmental Quality: 1970–2010

On January 1, 1970, President Richard Nixon signed the National Environmental Policy Act of 1969 (NEPA) into law. In this Act, Congress articulated for the first time a national policy on the environment. The goals of the Act included the promotion of "efforts to prevent or eliminate damage to the environment and biosphere and stimulate the health and welfare of man."[1] Congress also created the Council on Environment Quality (CEQ) to assist the president with the implementation of the new law and placed the new agency in the Executive Office of the President. The CEQ was to consist of three members, and it was to be supported by a professional staff selected by the CEQ.

On January 29, 1970, President Nixon nominated Russell E. Train to serve as the chair of the CEQ; he also nominated Robert Cahn and Gordon J. F. MacDonald to serve as the other members of the CEQ.[2] One week later, on February 6, 1970, the Senate confirmed the nominations, which officially allowed the new agency to open for business. In addition to ongoing consultations with the president and his advisors, Chairman Train and the other two members of the CEQ had to assemble a professional and administrative staff.

In August of 1970, only six months after the CEQ officially opened for business, President Nixon submitted *The First Annual Report of The Council on Environmental Quality* to Congress. The front section of the *Report* was "The President's Message to Congress." The remainder of the *Report*, developed by the CEQ, contained the first assessment of the nation's environment, a list of the underlying causes and effects of existing environmental problems, a review of the national government's efforts to address those problems over the previous two decades, and recommendations for improving environmental quality and protecting human health that involved changes in policy and administrative structure. It is especially noteworthy that the *Report* contained a section on the causes and effects of climate change, as well as recommendations for addressing this critical problem.[3]

In this chapter, we describe and attempt to explain what has happened to the CEQ over the forty-year period from 1970 to 2010. Our examination of the CEQ's life history will be focused on the agency's appropriations, a key factor that is often associated with the agency's capacity to carry out its statutorily assigned mission.

We begin our study with a brief review of the four different life cycle paths we might expect to see for an executive branch agency's appropriations. The schematic portraits of these four paths, which are predicted on the basis of the biological, partisan political, incremental, and issue-attention models, can be found in Figures 3.3, 3.4, 3.5, and 3.6, respectively.

In the second section of this chapter, we present the actual appropriations data for the CEQ, followed by some contextual background on what happened to the CEQ during each of the four decades between 1970 and 2010.

In the next part of the chapter, we compare the actual path of the CEQ's appropriations to the trajectory we expected to see on the basis of the predictions generated from the four life cycle models. As part of this comparison, we will report on the extent to which the path of the CEQ's actual appropriations between 1970 and 2010 fit the predictions generated from the four agency life cycle models.

FOUR PREDICTED PATHS FOR THE CEQ'S APPROPRIATIONS FROM 1970 TO 2010

Using the biological model as the basis for our predictions of the CEQ's appropriations, we would expect to see rapid growth in funding during the early years, followed by a long period of stable funding.

In contrast, using the partisan political model for our predictions, we would expect to see a wavelike pattern for the CEQ's appropriations after 1980. Specifically, beginning with Ronald Reagan's election to the presidency, we would expect to see appropriations go down under Republican presidents and Republican-controlled Congresses. We would expect to see appropriations rise under Democratic presidents and Congresses in which Democrats hold the majority.

On the basis of predictions generated by using the incremental model, we would expect to see a long, steady upward series of small increases in the CEQ's annual base appropriations. This long-term path, however, could be interrupted from time to time by incremental decreases in appropriations.

Using the issue-attention model as the basis for our predictions, we would expect to see a rapid rise in the CEQ's appropriations during the early years of its life cycle. Resources would begin to decline, however, after the first few years or so, as public attention and the attention of elected officials shift to other issues. Over the long term, the trend in appropriations would follow a wavelike trajectory as public and legislative attention to environmental problems rises and falls. The long-term direction of that wavelike pattern would be toward lower levels of resources.

CEQ APPROPRIATIONS AND STAFFING FROM FY 1970 TO FY 2010

The appropriations and staffing levels for the CEQ from FY 1970 through FY 2010 are presented in Figure 4.1. The darker of the two lines represents staff levels; the lighter of the two lines represents appropriations in inflation-adjusted or constant (2010) dollars. Funding and staff are both

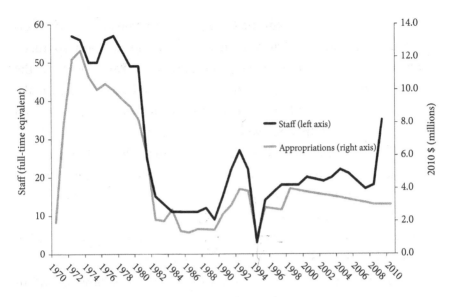

Figure 4.1 CEQ Staffing and Budget 1970–2010.

NOTES AND DATA SOURCE: Darker trend line shows staff levels (values on left axis); lighter trend line shows budget data, in 2010 dollars (values on right axis). Data from annual presidents' budgets: Office of Management and Budget, *Budget of the United States Government*, Federal Reserve Archives, http://fraser.stlouisfed.org/ publication/?pid=54. See Chapter 5, footnote 3, for details. The appropriations figure for 1970 is not directly comparable to the appropriations values for other years as it represents a partial year's spending (the CEQ was established during fiscal year 1970). The presidents' proposed budgets did not include actual figures for two years prior in the following cases: for appropriations in 2001 and for staff in 1970, 1971, 1986, and 2001. In these cases we interpolated in presenting the trend lines.

important elements of an agency's capacity to carry out the duties it is assigned in statutory law.

The level of appropriations is usually a key determinant of an agency's ability to hire and support staff. Given the small size of the CEQ's professional staff, however, resources were also used to pay for work performed through contracts by other organizations. In addition, the CEQ's staff was supplemented with detailees from other agencies, and a substantial amount of work was performed through interagency agreements.[4]

In this chapter our focus is on appropriations, but we think that the staff data are useful for representing what happened to the CEQ between 1970 and 2010. With the exception of 2009 and 2010, the two lines move in close correspondence.

As noted above, we present the CEQ's appropriations in constant dollars. We do so because that form has become the standard approach scholars take to examining agency appropriations. Participants in the budgetary process, however, including members of Congress, may make appropriations decisions that are focused on increases or decreases in an agency's base budget. In other words, they may use nominal dollars. If appropriations for the CEQ were presented in nominal dollars in Figure 4.1, appropriations would rise for the entire decade of the 1970s and through 1981. When constant 2010 dollars are used, however, the CEQ's appropriations decline after 1976.

All of the years presented in Figure 4.1 are fiscal years, and all references to appropriations throughout this chapter refer to fiscal years.

The data presented in Figure 4.1 show that the CEQ's appropriations (in constant 2010 dollars) reached a peak appropriation level of more than $12.5 million in 1973—only three years after the organization was created. Republican Richard Nixon was in office when Congress approved the funding for 1973. Over the three (fiscal) years in which Republican Gerald R. Ford occupied the presidency, however, resources declined by 13 percent and 7 percent in 1974 and 1975, respectively, before rising by 3 percent in 1975.

While President Jimmy Carter was in office, appropriations fell incrementally each year, dropping from approximately $10.5 million in 1976 to approximately $8.3 million in 1980. In comparison with subsequent trends, however, the CEQ's resources were sustained at a relatively high level during the Carter administration.

After the election of Republican Ronald Reagan in 1980, the CEQ's appropriations dropped dramatically. Specifically, in 1982 appropriations fell from a 1981 total of just under $8.3 million to approximately $2 million—a drop of 75 percent. Appropriations continued to fall between 1983 and 1986. The largest drop in those four years occurred in 1985, when the reduction was 25 percent of an already much diminished base budget. In 1989, Reagan's last budget, the CEQ's appropriations dropped below $1.5 million.

During Republican President George H.W. Bush's term, the CEQ's appropriations increased. In Bush's first budget year, 1990, appropriations rose by 67 percent. Then, appropriations rose by 20 percent and

33 percent, respectively, in 1991 and 1992. In 1992, appropriations reached a post-Reagan peak of almost $4 million.

In 1994, the first year Democratic President Bill Clinton submitted a budget request to Congress, appropriations for the CEQ fell by 86 percent to $0.5 million, the lowest level of any year after 1970. In 1995, however, appropriations rose by 159 percent, and they increased by 139 percent in 1997. Thus, by 1999, the CEQ's funding under Clinton exceeded the highest level of funding under President George H.W. Bush.

Under Republican President George W. Bush, the CEQ's appropriations stayed relatively flat between 2001 and 2005, but they dropped by 20 percent in 2006 and by 2 percent and 4 percent respectively in 2007 and 2008. In 2009, the CEQ's appropriations totaled $2.75 million.

During 2010, the first year in which Democrat Barack Obama submitted a budget request for the CEQ to Congress, appropriations rose 15 percent to almost $3.2 million.

Assuming that agency resources can serve as an indicator of the vigor of an organization, it appears that the CEQ was most active and influential during its first decade.[5] The agency then experienced an extended period of sharply reduced influence in the 1980s. After rebounding somewhat in the late 1980s and the first two years of the 1990s, the CEQ suffered a second major decline in the middle 1990s. Then, from 1995 to 2002 appropriations rose again, nearly reaching 1989 levels.

During the first four years of the George W. Bush administration, the CEQ's resources were relatively stable. Appropriations began to drop again after 2004, with a decrease of 20 percent in 2006 alone. Appropriations for 2009, the last fiscal year of the Bush administration, totaled almost $2.75 million.

As we discuss later in this chapter, however, the way in which the resources were used during George W. Bush's presidency was even more important than the appropriations levels. Specifically, the CEQ was used as a vehicle to block, slow, or reverse environmental protection and regulatory efforts. Thus, while the agency was not starved of resources, as it had been during the Reagan administration, its social function was significantly altered.

CONTEXTUAL CONSIDERATIONS: KEY EVENTS
BY DECADE AND ADMINISTRATION

In this section, some of the factors that may have caused, or at least contributed to, the CEQ's changing fortunes between 1970 and 2010 are presented on a decade-by-decade basis. Those factors include major events
taking place outside the governmental system, changes in the U.S. economy, presidential administrations, Congress, and the chairs of the CEQ.
In addition, some of the CEQ's important achievements during that time
period are described.

The 1970s: The First Decade

The CEQ quickly reached its highest levels of appropriations and staffing in the early 1970s, and the agency remained strong and influential
throughout the decade. President Nixon accepted a host of recommendations presented to him by the CEQ, including the creation of the Environmental Protection Agency (EPA) in 1970.[6] In doing so, President Nixon
was pursuing a strategy of co-optation, in which he focused on environmental issues that might otherwise have given political leverage to potential Democratic candidates in the 1972 election.

President Nixon also signed into law other major environmental legislation that the CEQ helped initiate, both before and after his reelection
in 1972. CEQ staff worked closely with the president and congressional
leaders from both political parties to advance the environmental agenda.[7]
A partial list of key environmental legislative actions during this period
includes the Clean Air Act in 1970; the Clean Water Act, the Marine
Mammal Protection Act, and the Coastal Zone Management Act in 1972;
and the Endangered Species Act in 1973.

It is also noteworthy that President Nixon appointed a strong leader to
serve as the first chair of the CEQ. Russell Train was a moderate Republican with a strong record of environmental advocacy. Train made sure
that President Nixon and his principal advisors were kept well informed

of CEQ activities. Chairman Train also actively engaged the press corps to help shape public opinion,[8] and he built an exceptionally capable staff of senior scientists at the agency, with wide experience in natural resource conservation and pollution control efforts.[9]

In 1973, after President Nixon nominated Russell Train to serve as the administrator for EPA, Nixon nominated Russell Peterson to replace Train as the CEQ's chair. Peterson not only had a Ph.D. in chemistry but also had served as governor of Delaware. President Gerald Ford kept Russell Peterson on as chair of the CEQ after Richard Nixon resigned the presidency. In 1977, however, Ford nominated John Busterud to be chair of the CEQ. Like Nixon, Ford continued to be responsive to the recommendations of the CEQ and its chair.[10]

President Jimmy Carter was elected with a strong commitment to the environment and broad support from environmental organizations. Although Carter initially considered merging the CEQ into the EPA, he gave up that idea relatively quickly and made two good appointments to chair the CEQ: Charles Warren, who served from 1977 to 1979, and Gus Speth, who served from 1979 to 1981. Warren and Speth were dedicated advocates for natural-resource conservation and pollution control, and they helped to drive the policy agenda in both areas. Speth also proved to be an adept leader.

The momentum generated during the early 1970s carried through the remainder of the decade, even though the "energy crisis" and rising economic and foreign policy concerns led to some decline in congressional and public support for action on the environment.[11] Important environmental laws passed during the Ford and Carter administrations include the Safe Drinking Water Act in 1974; the Toxic Substances Control Act, the Resource Conservation and Recovery Act, and the National Forest Management Act in 1976; the Surface Mining Control and Reclamation Act in 1977; and Superfund in 1980. While the CEQ continued to help develop these environmental laws, the responsibility for implementing and enforcing most of them fell to the EPA, which quickly grew into the largest regulatory authority in the federal government.

In addition to its important contributions to new environmental legislation, the CEQ's annual reports were profoundly influential during the

1970s and up to 1980. The data, analyses, and broad new ways of thinking about the relationship between society and the environment presented in these reports energized academic research and drove shifts worldwide in environmental policymaking.

In 1980, in collaboration with the Department of State, the CEQ completed a special report commissioned by President Carter entitled *The Global 2000 Report to the President: Entering the Twenty-First Century*.[12] With more than 1.5 million copies printed, this was one of the most popular and widely distributed government documents ever produced.

The Global 2000 Report included a farsighted early warning on climate change and a recommendation that prompt action be taken to reduce long-term risks from this threat. Although the *Report* stimulated public and press discussion of climate change, most presidents and most members of Congress who were in office between 1980 and 2010 largely ignored the recommendations.

Some of the key events in the life history of the CEQ, both in the 1970s and subsequent decades, are illustrated in Figure 4.2.

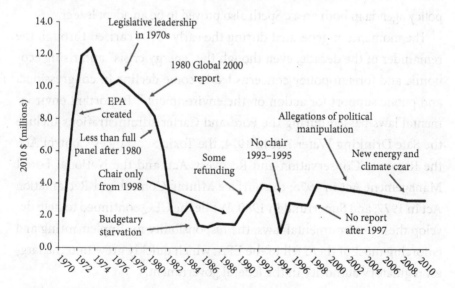

Figure 4.2 Key Events in the History of the CEQ.
NOTE: The trend line shows CEQ budget data in 2010 dollars.

The 1980s: The Second Decade

Shortly after publication of the *Global 2000 Report*, the CEQ entered a period of sharp decline. During the Reagan administration, the agency's 1982 budget and staff dropped to approximately 25 percent of 1980 levels and remained there until the end of President Reagan's two terms in office.

President Reagan nominated A. Alan Hill to be the CEQ's chair; he was confirmed by the Senate in 1981. Prior to his nomination, Hill had governmental experience in California's Agriculture Department, but his educational and environmental credentials were not comparable to those of previous CEQ chairs. In addition, from 1980 forward, the membership of the CEQ often fell below its full complement, as members who stepped down were not immediately replaced. Beginning in 1988, the last year of the Reagan administration, that pattern of not appointing members was formalized. From this time forward, the CEQ would consist only of a chair.[13]

Support for other environmental agencies, including the EPA, was also reduced during the Reagan years, but not nearly to the extent and duration felt by the CEQ. President Reagan's attack on environmental regulation ultimately triggered a political backlash that led to some restoration of the EPA's budget and authority in the mid-1980s. The CEQ, however, remained marginalized, and its funding declined in 1985 and 1986.

Continuing public concern for the environment helped shape the political dynamics of the 1988 election cycle. In part to distance himself from President Reagan, Vice President Bush promised in the campaign to lead a "kinder and gentler nation"[14] and to be an "environmental president."[15]

After his election in November of 1988, President George H.W. Bush appointed Michael R. Deland to serve as the CEQ's chair. Deland previously served as Regional Administrator for Region 1 in the EPA from 1983 to 1989, during the Reagan administration. During President Bush's term, funding for the CEQ rose from the very low levels of the Reagan administration to almost half of what it had been at the end of the Carter administration.

The 1990s: The Third Decade

President George H.W. Bush's agenda shifted as the 1992 elections approached. He resisted action on global climate change, for example, and strictly limited U.S. involvement in the 1992 Earth Summit in Rio de Janeiro. He also famously disparaged vice-presidential candidate Al Gore's environmental leanings, labeling him "Ozone Man."[16] Despite this shift, the CEQ had more funding at the end of the president's term than it had four years earlier.

During the first two years of the Clinton administration, the CEQ reached its nadir. As part of his "reinventing government" agenda,[17] President Clinton planned to abolish the CEQ and pass its duties to the EPA, which in turn would be elevated to a cabinet department. Caldwell[18] and Bear[19] describe this proposed bureaucratic realignment as representing a clear misreading of NEPA requirements and a profound misunderstanding of the CEQ's statutory purpose.

From 1993 to 1994, while these changes were being debated, President Clinton did not appoint a chair for the CEQ. Since no members other than the chair had been seated since 1988, the CEQ effectively ceased to exist. A skeleton staff of fewer than five people remained at work in the CEQ offices. Once Congress made it clear that it would not approve Clinton's plan to create a Department of the Environment, however, the President appointed Kathleen McGinty, a former staff member to Vice President Al Gore, to serve as the chair of the CEQ. Clinton also returned the agency to the budget and staffing levels it had at the beginning of his term.

In the meantime, however, the strongly antiregulatory Republican majority elected in November of 1994 acted rapidly and aggressively in the 1995 session of Congress on its promise to shrink government. Led in the House of Representatives by Newt Gingrich, Republicans used several tactics to pursue their agenda. One tactic was to take actions that appeared to be innocuous but actually had a profound impact on current and potential future regulatory activity.

One legislative action of this type was The Paperwork Reduction Act of 1995.[20] The Act was purportedly designed to reduce the number of superfluous government reports. Under that Act, however, the CEQ's annual report on the environment was one of about forty agency reports that Gingrich and the 104th Congress specifically identified as superfluous, despite unequivocal language in NEPA requiring the production of this report. Consequently, the CEQ's 1997 *Annual Report of the Council on Environmental Quality* was its last.

Kathleen McGinty resigned as CEQ chair in 1998. President Clinton's new nominee to serve as chair was George Frampton, who previously served as the Assistant Secretary of the Interior for Fish and Wildlife. Frampton served as CEQ chair from 1998 to the end of Clinton's term.

2000–2010: The Fourth Decade

While the Clinton administration either misunderstood or ignored NEPA's original intent for the CEQ during its first two years in office, it appears that the George W. Bush administration acted to reverse the social function specified for the agency in NEPA. President Bush pursued a strong antiregulatory agenda that included efforts on many fronts to reduce constraints that environmental regulations imposed on the private sector. These policies included delaying action on climate change, reducing regulation of older coal-fired power plants, providing stronger incentives for energy exploration and production, and increasing timber harvesting in national forests. The CEQ was given the task of promoting and justifying these policies.

President George W. Bush's CEQ chair throughout his presidency was James Connaughton. In a 2008 interview, Connaughton described his understanding of the role of the Council as follows: "The CEQ's job is to ensure that the president's philosophy and policies are being effectively implemented throughout the government."[21]

Yet the mandate assigned to the CEQ and its chair in NEPA seems to be quite different from the one Connaughton articulated. The statutory language includes the following provision: "It shall be the duty and function of the Council . . . to review and appraise the various programs and activities of the Federal Government in the light of the policy set forth in

Title I of this Act for the purpose of determining the extent to which such programs are contributing to the achievement of such policy, and to make recommendations to the President with respect thereto."

In NEPA, Congress set forth a far-reaching, long-term national policy to protect and preserve the environment and human health. In NEPA, Congress also requires the CEQ to assess progress toward achieving the goals laid out in the statement of that policy and to advise the president on how to strengthen the government's efforts to that end. Chairman Connaughton's view, however, was that the CEQ's responsibility was to promote the president's philosophy and policies, without reference to the larger national policy articulated in NEPA.

In 2005, the CEQ was drawn into controversy as *The New York Times* reported that Philip Cooney, the CEQ's chief of staff, who had no scientific training, edited government climate reports "to play up uncertainty or play down evidence of a human role in global warming."[22] Immediately before coming to the CEQ, Cooney worked for the American Petroleum Institute, the oil industry's primary lobby in Washington, D.C. Following these disclosures, Cooney resigned from the CEQ and was hired by ExxonMobil. In 2007, when he was called before a House committee investigating the Bush administration's alleged political interference in climate science, Cooney defended himself against accusations of favoring oil interests during his time at the CEQ by testifying that "my sole loyalties were to the president."[23]

In October of 2008, just one month before Barack Obama was elected to the presidency, many former CEQ chairs, members, and senior staff from Republican and Democratic administrations over the previous three decades met to prepare a memorandum for the incoming administration. The group's key recommendation was that the new president give the CEQ a lead role on the environment, particularly on climate change, and give the CEQ the financial and staffing resources necessary to fill that role effectively. The report concluded:

We are in the midst of the second great environmental crisis. The first rose in the 1960s and resulted in a remarkable new statute and an equally remarkable new office, the Council on Environmental Quality. They have proven their worth. We are now facing a crisis

that dwarfs the previous one, with many of the old problems yet un-
solved. CEQ was intended to be a leading part of the solution, and it
should be now as well.[24]

Rather than assigning the lead role on climate change to the CEQ, however, President Obama created a new position on the White House staff
for an energy and climate change "czar," and he named Carol Browner
to that position. Browner had strong credentials for the position, having
served as EPA administrator under President Clinton.

President Obama's nominee to head the CEQ was Nancy Sutley, a
former deputy mayor of Los Angeles. Sutley had a good track record, but
she had a much lower political profile than Carol Browner. Given the difference in rank and reputation between Browner and Sutley, one might
conclude that President Obama and his key White House staff members
decided against making the CEQ a "leading part of the solution" to the
"second great environmental crisis." On the other hand, the fact that the
CEQ's appropriations rose by 15 percent in 2010 in Obama's first budget
is one indication that the agency would not be completely marginalized.
Additionally, the CEQ's staff grew by more than 50 percent in 2010.

COMPARING THE ACTUAL LIFE CYCLE PATH
TO THE PREDICTED PATH

Having summarized what happened to the CEQ's appropriations between 1970 and 2010 and having reviewed some of the key events and circumstances related to the CEQ's life cycle trajectory over that forty-year
period of time, we will now turn our attention to an examination of the
relative fit between the predicted path of the CEQ's appropriations trajectory and its actual path. Specifically, we will compare the actual path of
the CEQ's resources presented in Figure 4.1 to the path predicted using
the biological, partisan political, incremental, and issue-attention models
and presented in Figures 3.3, 3.4, 3.5, and 3.6 respectively.

On the basis of that comparison, a number of general findings can be
reported. First, the actual path of the CEQ's appropriations *does not fit* the

predicted path generated from any one of the four life cycle models over the entire forty years between 1970 and 2010.

Second, during various segments of time, the actual path of the CEQ's appropriations *does fit* the path predicted by one (or more) of the models. Furthermore, during those segments of time, the key variables identified in each model seem to work effectively to explain what happened to the CEQ. For example, the rapid rise in the CEQ's appropriations path during the early years of its existence fits the path we predicted using both the biological and the issue-attention models. In addition, the CEQ's appropriations path during the Reagan administration fit the path predicted using the partisan political model.

Third, during some time segments the CEQ's actual appropriations moved in a direction (up or down) that was the opposite of, or at least contrary to, the path predicted on the basis of at least one of the models. In the case of the partisan political model, for example, the CEQ's appropriation rose, rather than fell, under Republican President George H.W. Bush (1989–1992). Likewise, appropriations fell, rather than rose, during the first two years (1993–1994) of Democratic President Bill Clinton's administration.

Fourth, the poor fit between the CEQ's actual appropriations and predictions generated by one life cycle model can, in some cases, be explained, at least in part, by employing another life cycle model. Finally, during some segments of time, the CEQ's appropriations path fit the path predicted by one model, but the explanatory variables of that model did not fit the circumstances. In such cases, the explanatory variable from another model seemed a better fit.

Examples of a Good Fit Between Actual Appropriations and Predictions

Here is some additional detail on each of the examples in which the fit between the CEQ's appropriations closely fit a path predicted by at least one of the models. During the early 1970s, the CEQ's appropriations grew rapidly, as predicted on the basis of the biological model (Fig. 3.1). In addition, the resources and influence of the organization grew rapidly, and the young agency seemed to have successfully passed through the *critical survival threshold* identified by Anthony Downs (1967).

The key "internal" variables in the biological model that seem to have contributed to the rapid growth in resources for the new agency included (1) an energetic and effective leader of the CEQ who was strongly committed to the social functions established in NEPA and (2) the impressive results that were achieved by the agency during that period of time. Among the "external" factors that contributed to these results was the strong support members of both political parties in Congress gave the CEQ.

The predictions developed from the issue-attention cycle also seem to fit the early years of the CEQ's existence. The key "external" factors that would help to explain the rapid growth in resources include the dramatic rise in public concern about environmental problems in the late 1960s and early 1970s and the way in which members of Congress responded to the public's demand for solutions to these problems.

During the 1980s, the actual trajectory of the agency's appropriations seems to closely match the path predicted on the basis of the partisan political model. President Reagan explicitly articulated a pro-business, antigovernment, antiregulatory ideology. The CEQ's new chair was a party loyalist, the agency's resources were cut back sharply, and its vigor in pursuit of the social functions defined in NEPA dropped off significantly. Thus, during the Reagan presidency, and during most of the agency's second decade, the actual trajectory of the agency seems to closely match the path predicted on the basis of the partisan political model.

During the period of time from 1998 through 2005, the predictions developed on the basis of the incremental model seem to correspond closely to what happened to the CEQ's resources. Appropriations were relatively stable, with a series of incremental increases in five of the seven years, no change in one year, and two years in which the base budget declined by 2 percent. Over the full eight years, appropriations grew by 9.1 percent.

Of these examples, the partisan political model seems to fit, or serve as a predictor for, what is arguably the most important event in the CEQ's overall life cycle between 1970 and 2010. Specifically, by attempting to kill the agency and by ensuring that the CEQ's resources were slashed in 1982, President Reagan and his senior advisors reset the CEQ's trajectory for the next thirty years. The CEQ's resources, like the agency's role and status within the Executive Office of the President and the governmental system as a whole, never fully recovered from those crushing blows.

Appropriations Contrary to Expectations

While the partisan political model is a perfect fit for what happened to the CEQ's appropriations during the Reagan administration, the actual path of the CEQ's resources could be described as the opposite of the path predicted on the basis of that model during the presidential terms of Republican George H.W. Bush and the first two years of Democratic President Bill Clinton's term.

During President George H.W. Bush's term, appropriations rose by 67 percent in 1990, 20 percent in 1991, and 33 percent in 1992. One consequence was that appropriations reached a post-Reagan peak of almost $4 million in 1992. During President Clinton's first two years in office, the CEQ's appropriations fell to their lowest levels, with an 86 percent decline in 1994.

A third time segment in which the actual path of the CEQ's appropriations was contrary to the path predicted by the partisan political model was during the first term of the George W. Bush administration. Appropriations remained relatively stable, instead of dropping, between 2001 and 2004.

The discovery of the mismatch between the actual appropriations path and the path predicted on the basis of the partisan political model is important, but it is equally important to find the explanation for what happened during these time segments. For example, the 67 percent increase in appropriations during George H.W. Bush's term was the result of decisions made by Democrats in Congress. President Bush did not ask for the increase, but Democratic majorities in both the House and Senate decided to appropriate the additional funding for the CEQ. Thus, it appears that the partisan political model applies for this particular year, but Congress, rather than the president, was the driving force.

In the section below, an examination of why appropriations dropped, rather than rose, under President Clinton in 1993 and 1994 is provided. Then, in the next section, a review of the circumstances in which appropriations remained stable, rather than fell, during George W. Bush's term is presented.

Using Alternative Life Cycle Models to Describe and Explain Appropriations

In Chapter 3 and in the beginning of this chapter, we emphasized the fact that we generated four different, or even competing, predictions for an executive branch organization's appropriations path. Those predictions were based on the biological, partisan political, incremental, and issue-attention life cycle models. Thus, even though the predictions made on the basis of one model may not fit what actually happened during a particular segment of time, we may find that another model can be used to describe and explain what happened in that particular time segment.

For example, the biological model could be used to describe and explain what took place with respect to the substantial reduction in the CEQ's appropriations between 1993 and 1994 under Democratic President Clinton. As reported in Chapter 3, in the discussion of the biological model, Anthony Downs contends that all executive branch agencies have "functional" and "allocational" rivals. Functional rivals are competitors for an agency's social mission, and they can exist inside or outside the executive branch. Allocational rivals are competitors for scarce resources. Traditionally, the key allocational rivals have been other government agencies.[25]

President Clinton's efforts to make the EPA a cabinet department and, in the process, eliminate the CEQ could be considered the result of the (potential) underlying competition for dominance in the social mission between the CEQ and the EPA. Clinton's move could also be explained on the basis of a (potential) competition between the two organizations for resources. While Downs indicated that such competition could be fatal for a new agency, he also noted the possibility of such competition flaring up in later stages in an agency's life cycle.

Challenges Associated with Using a Single Model to Describe and Explain Appropriations

In a previous section, the gap between the expected and actual path of the CEQ's appropriations during President George W. Bush's term was reported. Specifically, the CEQ's appropriations did not fall, as predicted by the partisan political model, between 2001 and 2005. Instead, appropriations remained relatively stable. Consequently, it appears that the incremental model, rather than the partisan political model, is a good fit for describing the CEQ's appropriations path between 2001 and 2004.

The incremental model is not a useful tool, however, for explaining the appropriations path between 2001 and 2004. The CEQ's path was not based on inertia, and it was not the result of "protection" provided through a relatively closed decision-making system involving the CEQ, the Office of Management and Budget, Congressional appropriations committees, and interest groups committed to protecting the environment and human health.

The CEQ's funding was sustained, rather than cut, by the White House because the CEQ was being used as a tool for partisan political purposes. In sharp contrast to the social purposes defined for the agency in NEPA, the CEQ's focus under President George W. Bush was on slowing, stopping, or even reversing the development and implementation of environmental laws. Given the fact that Bush offered a pro-business and antiregulatory agenda that seemed to parallel Ronald Reagan's, this finding may not be surprising. The finding does highlight, however, some of the challenges associated with drawing a conclusion about the fit between an agency's actual appropriations path and the path predicted on the basis of a particular life cycle model.

Bush showed malleability – but not necessarily in the spirit of the law

The Environmental Protection Agency: 1970–2010

The official birthdate of the U.S. Environmental Protection Agency (EPA) is December 2, 1970. On that day the Senate confirmed William Ruckelshaus, President Nixon's nominee to be the administrator of the new agency, and the "EPA opened for business in a tiny suite of offices at 20th and L Streets in Northwest Washington, DC."[1] The new agency took over programs and offices related to environmental protection previously operating in the Department of the Interior, the Department of Agriculture, the Department of Health, Education, and Welfare, the Food and Drug Administration, the Atomic Energy Commission, and the Federal Radiation Council.

In this chapter, we examine and attempt to explain what happened to this major regulatory agency over the forty-year period from its birth in 1970 to 2010. In doing so, we test hypotheses that follow from the four categories of theoretical agency life cycle models introduced in Chapter 3.

These models differ in their predictions for the trajectories of federal agencies. The biological model predicts that agencies will grow rapidly during their early life before reaching a relatively stable maturity. Over subsequent decades agencies may carry on indefinitely with declining vigor, or be absorbed into other agencies, or die, although scholars debate both the process and probability of agency mortality.[2]

The partisan political model predicts a more turbulent life history for agencies in which changing party control of Congress and the White House will buffet government organizations more or less routinely. According to this model, federal agencies will often be caught in the middle of partisan ideological battles over the importance and value of the social functions they were created to address.

The incremental model suggests that the best predictor of how agencies will fare in the near future is how they have fared in the recent past. That is, agencies tend to be insulated from external political and economic fluctuations and therefore generally experience relatively minor changes over time to their budgets and operations.

The issue-attention model predicts that agencies' fortunes are tied to the vagaries of current events. That is, when a concern captures public attention, the media will fan interest in the topic, thereby generating a positive feedback loop that elevates the problem on the national agenda. Politicians will respond, providing bursts of support and demands for action to the agencies with social functions most relevant to the issue at hand. Then, inevitably, public interest and attention will wane, and the agencies will fall back to their prior states.

In the case of the EPA, our principal indicator of the agency's vitality and influence is its operating budget, which includes core activities such as research, regulation, enforcement, and facilities management but excludes expenditures for Superfund and for grants or revolving-fund outlays to states, municipalities, and tribes. In measuring the EPA's budget in this way, we follow the lead of other scholars who have studied the agency.[3] When discussing budgets in particular years we are referring to fiscal years.

In this chapter, we describe our efforts to explain changes in the EPA's operating budget using three methods. Our first approach involves predicting general development paths for the agency following from the four

theoretical models introduced above and then considering qualitative assessments of the fit of the observed trajectory of the EPA to the paths
predicted by the theories. Our second approach involves conducting
quantitative analyses testing hypothesized relationships between trends
for the EPA's budget and changes in various political, economic, and social
variables that can be expected to influence support for the agency over
time. Our third approach involves supplementing these qualitative and
quantitative assessments of the overall forty-year life history of the EPA
with more narrowly focused case studies of selected fiscal years in which
the EPA experienced unusually large changes in its budget, either positive
or negative, compared to the years immediately prior. Before reviewing
the predictions of the theoretical models and describing the results of our
empirical analyses and case studies, we begin with a brief review of the
political and historical context for the establishment of the EPA.

POLITICAL AND HISTORICAL CONTEXT

The environment was high on the national agenda in the late 1960s and
early 1970s. In December 1969 Congress passed the National Environmental Policy Act, which established the Council on Environmental
Quality (CEQ). In January 1970 President Nixon used his State of the
Union address to propose making "the 1970s an historic period when, by
conscious choice, we transform our land into what we want it to become."[4]
In April 1970 millions of people across the country participated in the
first Earth Day celebrations. In July the president submitted an executive-
branch reorganization plan to the House of Representatives that included
creating the EPA.[5] Congress signaled its favorable response, and the EPA
came into being in December 1970.

President Nixon's formal comments justifying the creation of the EPA
are of particular interest given this book's focus on agency life cycles. In
establishing the EPA, the president noted that he was making an exception to one of his key principles, that "as a matter of effective and orderly
administration, additional new independent agencies normally should

not be created."[6] This statement reflects a deeply rooted conservative tradition in American political history favoring constraints on the growth of bureaucracy.

Among the reasons the president offered for overriding this principle was that "concern with the condition of our physical environment has intensified."[7] This comment reveals a political sensitivity to both emerging public activism on the environment and the energetic way in which Congress was developing new environmental legislation.[8] Part of the president's motivation in promoting his own environmental agenda was to co-opt an issue that might otherwise have served as a strong platform for potential Democratic presidential challengers in the upcoming elections of 1972.[9]

Two other reasons President Nixon offered for his actions were based on rationales for government reorganization that are commonly noted in the field of public administration. He wrote that "Government's environmentally-related activities have grown up piecemeal over the years" and that the time had "come to organize" those activities "rationally and systematically."[10] In particular, the president asserted that "As no disjointed array of separate programs can, the EPA would be able—in concert with the States—to set and enforce standards for air and water quality and for individual pollutants."[11]

The president thus framed his justification for creating the EPA in the language of New Federalism, an approach in favor at the time aimed at promoting efficiency in the national government while devolving appropriate authorities to the states. The political reality of high public concern for the environment led him to create the EPA and lead an energetic environmental legislative agenda, but his conservative roots led him to do so using the language of limited government and states' rights.

Thus the EPA was born in a time of broad bipartisan support for strong new regulations to promote public health and protect the environment. Over the course of the next forty years, however, public and political support for the agency waxed and waned. By the early 1980s, more polarized attitudes toward environmental protection in general, and the EPA in particular, had replaced the bipartisan consensus of the 1970s. During some periods, including the late 1980s and early 1990s, a measure of broad support reemerged, but at other times, including the presidential election cycles of 2008 and 2012, polarization returned and partisan attacks on the EPA as a "job-killer" intensified.[12] As noted in the agency's history posted on the EPA's own website, "Few federal agencies evoke as much emotion in the average American as the US Environmental Protection Agency."[13]

GENERAL QUALITATIVE PREDICTIONS FROM AGENCY LIFE CYCLE THEORIES

We use the four categories of theoretical agency life cycle models introduced previously to frame our discussion of the EPA in this chapter: the biological model, the partisan political model, the incremental model, and the issue-attention model. In this section we examine the fit between expectations based on the four models and the actual trajectory of the EPA's budget over time.

Using the biological model to make a rough qualitative prediction of the EPA's budgetary history, we would expect to see rapid early growth, followed by an extended period of relative stability, degenerating ultimately to stagnation and decline. In contrast, using the partisan political model we would expect to see a contingent, wavelike path for the EPA's budget. Given the stereotypical ideologies of the two parties in this simple model, we would expect to see a pattern of increases during periods of Democratic Party ascendancy and declines during periods of Republican Party ascendancy. Recognizing the increased polarization of the parties that began with the election of Ronald Reagan in 1980, we would expect shifts in party control in Washington to generate greater variation in the EPA's budget since that time. Figures 3.3 and 3.4 in Chapter 3 present these hypothesized trajectories schematically.

A rough qualitative prediction based on the incremental model would lead us to expect a long-term trend of modest variations for the agency's budget around a well-established and relatively stable baseline. The issue-attention model, on the other hand, would predict sharp increases in the agency's budget when the public and mass media focus on environmental issues, followed by declines to prior levels as interest wanes and public and media attention turns to other matters. Figures 3.5 and 3.6 in Chapter 3 present these trajectories.

Figure 5.1 presents actual trends in nominal and inflation-adjusted budgetary authority for the EPA for fiscal years 1970 to 2010.[14] The darker line represents the inflation-adjusted values (in 2010 dollars), and the lighter line represents nominal values. We present the nominal trend, even though inflation-adjusted values are more appropriate for visualizing changes in dollar values over time, because elected officials are likely to consider nominal dollar values when making budgetary decisions. Also, a comparison of the trend lines highlights the distorting effects of inflation. For example, in 1980 and 1981, the two years following the vertical reference line at 1979, real declines in the EPA's budget during the period of high inflation following the second oil shock appear as increases in nominal values. Thus the sharp declines in the EPA's budget in the

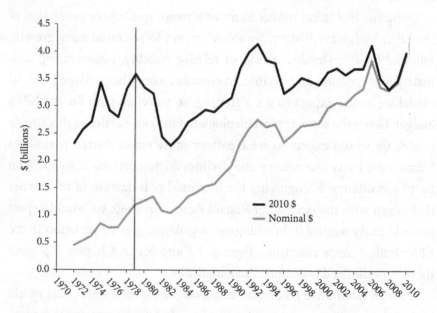

Figure 5.1 **EPA Budget 1970–2010, Nominal and Inflation-Adjusted (2010 dollars).**
DATA SOURCE: See footnote 3 for details.

early 1980s actually started in the Carter administration rather than in the Reagan administration, as usually reported.

In comparing qualitative predictions from the four theoretical models of agency life cycles to the actual path of the EPA, we use the inflation-adjusted budget numbers in Figure 5.1 as the measure of the agency's trajectory. The biological model predicts a period of rapid growth followed by a long-lasting plateau in which the mature agency experiences modest changes to an established budgetary base. This prediction fits best with the EPA's startup phase. Here we see a steep increase from 1970 to 1975, by which time the agency appears to have passed the initial survival stage to become well established.

The years from 1975 to 2010 can be seen overall as a period of slow growth, with the inflation-adjusted budget in 2010 only 16 percent higher than in 1975. However, the intermediate changes over this period were hardly modest and rarely resembled a flat plateau. In real terms, the EPA's budget dropped by approximately 35 percent from 1979 to 1983. It then rose 80 percent in ten years of strong growth to a high point in 1993, before dropping back by more than 20 percent over the next three years. Despite an increasing workload, the agency's budget was about 4 percent lower in 2010 than at its peak in 1993. The relatively stable mature stage for an agency predicted by the biological model fails to capture this volatility.

The partisan political model, in contrast, assumes volatility. It predicts that the EPA's budget will rise in times of Democratic Party control and fall in times of Republican Party control. There are several periods in which this model appears to anticipate the observed variations. For example, the agency's budget rose in the early years of the Carter, Clinton, and Obama administrations and fell during early years of the Reagan administration. Moreover, the decline in the middle of President Clinton's first term coincided with the so-called Gingrich revolution in which Republicans gained control of the House of Representatives for the first time in forty years. William Ruckelshaus, writing during this time, used the metaphor of a pendulum swinging back and forth to describe changes in the EPA's budget over time, with each swing representing a backlash to the previous period of proregulatory or antiregulatory fervor.[15]

On the other hand, several periods do not match well with the predictions of the partisan political model. The years of strongest growth for the agency occurred under Republican presidents Nixon, Ford, and George H.W. Bush. Even during parts of the Reagan and George W. Bush administrations the agency fared better than might be expected. In the first two fiscal years of the Reagan administration, 1982 and 1983, the EPA's budget declined dramatically. In 1983, however, EPA Administrator Gorsuch resigned under pressure after being cited for contempt of Congress. Following this period of turmoil, William Ruckelshaus returned to the EPA's top position, and the agency's inflation-adjusted budget increased in five of the remaining six years of the Reagan administration. During the George W. Bush administration the EPA's inflation-adjusted budget was relatively stable, with an overall increase over the first five fiscal years, 2002 through 2006, before experiencing more volatility later in the president's second term.

The incremental model does not account for an agency's startup period but rather considers the likely trajectory of an established organization. This model can be interpreted as making predictions for an agency's path that are similar to those of the extended mature stage of the biological model between birth and decline. Thus the comparisons between the predicted and observed paths of the EPA from 1975 to 2010 based on the biological model apply to the incremental model as well. As noted above, a macro-scale view of the agency's inflation-adjusted budget over the thirty-five-year period reveals a modest overall increase, in keeping with the predictions of incrementalism. However, the intermediate dramatic increases and decreases in the agency's fortunes are too great to be fairly described as incremental.

The issue-attention model predicts sharp increases in an agency's budget when issues included in the agency's portfolio rise on the national agenda. The model predicts that as interest in the topic later subsides, resources allocated to the agency will decline to prior levels. The trajectory of the EPA illustrated in Figure 5.1 over the first twenty-five years of our study period fits the model relatively well. Public interest in the environment was high in the early 1970s when the EPA was born and flourished. By the end of the Carter administration and in the early years of the Reagan administration, other concerns related to foreign affairs and the economy had displaced the environment on the political agenda. Hostages in Iran, oil shocks, stagflation, and recession, along with some improvement in environmental conditions and rising concern about the costs of environmental regulation, dampened enthusiasm for further action. As the issue-attention model predicts, the EPA's budget dropped substantially in this period.

In the mid-1980s, the environment again became an important issue, both nationally and internationally. At the time of the 1988 presidential election, as indicated in Figure 5.2, public opinion data from two major surveys showed that public support for environmental action in the United States was approaching a high point.[16] Responding to voter interest, the candidates attacked each other's environmental credentials. Candidate Bush, for example, attempted to score political points against

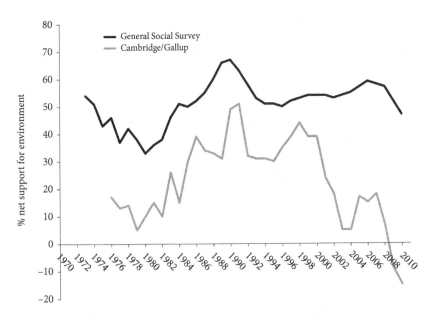

Figure 5.2 Public Opinion Polling on the Environment.
DATA SOURCES: See footnotes 29 and 30 for details. Darker trend line shows data from General Social Survey; lighter trend line shows data from Cambridge and Gallup.

Michael Dukakis, his Democratic challenger, by accusing him of having failed as governor of Massachusetts to clean up Boston Harbor.[17]

At the international level, plans were under way for the so-called Earth Summit, to be held in Rio de Janeiro in 1992. As predicted by the issue-attention model, the EPA's budget rose substantially during this period. In 1993 the agency's budget reached its highest point in real terms. As also predicted by the issue-attention model, however, the political winds in the United States soon shifted and the agency's budget fell back. President Bush, who had promised in the campaign of 1988 to be an "environmental president,"[18] was in 1992 broadly criticized for his failure to support global action on environmental protection at the summit in Brazil.[19]

For the remaining years of our study period, the issue-attention model does less well. As indicated in Figure 5.2, public opinion polling on the environment gives inconsistent results after the late 1990s. Also the trajectory of the EPA's budget presented in Figure 5.1 does not show large declines in spending on the environment that the issue-attention model might predict as other major events, such as the attacks of September 11, 2001, and the deep recession that began in 2008, captured public attention and affected the national agenda.

On the basis of these initial qualitative assessments, none of the four theoretical agency life cycle models generates predictions that hold up well over the entire history of the EPA. Qualitatively the issue-attention model appears to match reasonably closely with the actual trajectory of the agency for about two thirds of the time period we studied. The other three models are substantially less successful in predicting outcomes.

A REVIEW OF OUR QUANTITATIVE FINDINGS

In this section, we describe our efforts to test the theories more rigorously. We discuss the results of our empirical analyses aimed at explaining changes in the EPA's budget over time and consider the implications of our findings for the agency life cycle models.

The Annual Change in the EPA's Budget as the Variable To Be Explained

Figure 5.3 presents data for the EPA's inflation-adjusted budgetary authority granted by Congress from 1973 to 2010 in the form of the percent
change from the previous year.[20] A bar above the zero line indicates a positive change in the EPA's budget, and a bar below the zero line indicates a
negative change. In our analysis, we use the data presented in Figure 5.3
as the variable to be explained—that is, the dependent variable.

Transforming the data to the percent change from the previous year
from the inflation-adjusted dollar values presented in Figure 5.1 has
two benefits. The first is methodological, in that it minimizes the adverse effects on the analysis of inflationary and noninflationary growth
over time and associated violations of assumptions underlying statistical
techniques.[21] The second is conceptual, in that what we actually want to
explain is the change in budgetary authority from one year to the next,
rather than the dollar value of the budget in a given year.

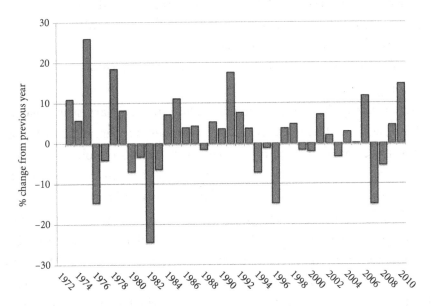

**Figure 5.3 EPA Budget 1973–2010, Percent Change from Previous Year
(Inflation-Adjusted).**
DATA SOURCE: See footnote 3 for details.

The average percent change from the previous fiscal year in the inflation-adjusted budget for the EPA is +1.9 percent. While the distribution is approximately normal (see Chapter 7, Fig. 7.1), there is a high degree of variation around the average.[22] The maximum annual increase is 26 percent in 1975, and the maximum decrease is 24 percent in 1982. While these are the only two values that might formally be considered outliers,[23] there are six other years in which the annual change is 15 percent or greater, either positive or negative.

Variables that Might Explain the Changes in the EPA's Budget

Following other researchers, we examine various political, economic, and social indicators to see if they can help us understand the changes that have occurred in the EPA's budget over time.[24] The political variables focus on the federal legislative and executive branches. In our analysis, we experiment with various combinations of variables measuring party control of the presidency and party membership in, and control of, each house of Congress. For economic variables, we test such factors as the unemployment rate, the rate of growth or decline in gross domestic product, and the rate of change in overall federal nondefense discretionary spending.[25]

In including the variable for nondefense discretionary spending, we follow the ideas of political scientist Christopher Wlezien. He reports that social policy areas may be aggregated in the minds of voters and their elected representatives. He writes that policymakers in making budgets may "respond to a general preference for government action broadly defined, in effect, *across* various policy areas" rather than more narrowly "to public preferences *within* particular areas" (emphasis in original).[26] He finds, for example, that spending preferences for the environment tend to move together with those for welfare, education, health, and urban issues. He also describes a "guns-butter trade-off" in which budgetary pressures for social priorities are typically inversely related to movements in national defense budgets.[27] Thus, we include the variable for nondefense discretionary spending in our analysis to examine whether the EPA's budget tends to move together with overall social spending in this way.

We also explore the effects on the EPA's budget of changes in public attitudes toward the environment. The issue-attention model assumes that public attitudes help drive government action. Wlezien's research also supports incorporating this variable. He suggests that public opinion may act as a "thermostat" to moderate budgetary fluctuations.[28] That is, greater public concern for, and willingness to spend money on, a salient policy issue induces policymakers to increase appropriations in that area. Then as spending rises, public pressure for additional expenditures in that policy realm wanes, discouraging further increases. In this view, public opinion related to a policy area and actual appropriations in that area affect each other in a cyclical manner, tending to maintain relative budgetary stability.

To test the effect of public opinion, we use two alternate measures of public concern for the environment. The first is based on responses to a question included in the General Social Survey asking respondents whether they think the country is spending "too much," "too little," or "about the right amount" on the environment. The question appeared in the survey for twenty-seven of the forty years in the time period of our study. We include this variable in our analysis as net public support for more spending on the environment, computed by subtracting the percentage responding "too much" from the percentage responding "too little" and then converting to percent change in this value from the prior year.[29]

A second way of measuring public opinion on the environment is to ask whether respondents prioritize environmental protection over economic growth or vice versa. Cambridge polling asked a question on this topic from 1976 to 1990. Gallup polling asked a similar question from 1991 to 2010. In combination, these polls provide data for thirty-one of the forty years of our study period. We include this variable in our analysis as net public support for environmental protection, computed by subtracting the percentage prioritizing economic growth from the percentage prioritizing environmental protection and then converting to percent change in this value from the prior year.[30]

Figure 5.2 displays trends in these two ways of gauging public support for the environment. The darker line represents results from the General Social Survey computed as the percentage of respondents saying we're spending too much on the environment subtracted from the percentage saying we're spending too little. The lighter line represents results from Cambridge (1976–1990) and Gallup (1991–2010) computed as the percentage of respondents saying economic growth should be given priority over environmental protection subtracted from the percentage saying environmental protection should be given priority over economic growth.

As Figure 5.2 illustrates, the two measures are in accord in indicating that for most of the period of our study the public generally prioritized the environment over the economy and favored spending more on the environment than was currently being spent. Figure 5.2 also reveals that the two polling approaches agree on the general shape of the trends from the mid-1970s to the late 1990s, with both indicating a low point in public support for the environment around 1980 and a high point around 1990.[31]

The two measures diverge significantly over the final decade, however. The General Social Survey results show only relatively minor variations in public attitudes on environmental spending from 1999 to 2010. On the other hand, Gallup polling on the prioritization of the environment over the economy indicates a steep drop beginning in 1999 that actually becomes negative in 2009 and 2010—meaning that for the first time more respondents prioritized economic growth over environmental protection, likely as a consequence of the severe recession that began in 2008.

Expectations and Limitations

Given common-sense intuitions about factors that may affect budgets for federal agencies and the qualitative predictions of the theoretical models, we hypothesize that more Democratic Party control in Washington, better national economic performance, higher rates of overall government nondefense discretionary spending, and higher levels of public support for environmental protection will correlate with higher budgets for the EPA. We note that some interpretations of the incremental model predict that agency budgets will move more or less randomly around established baselines, largely insulated from social, political, and economic influences. If this is so, we might expect not to find any relationships between changes in the EPA's budget and patterns in the movements of other variables.

Two characteristics of the data limit the power of our analysis. First, the time period of our study is relatively short.[32] Second, the change in the agency's budget, the variable we are trying to explain, varies widely from year to year. The relatively small size of the dataset and the relatively large variation in the key variable we are studying both tend to reduce the likelihood of finding significant results.

Results and Discussion for the Quantitative Analysis

None of the political or economic variables we tested shows an association with the observed pattern of annual changes in the EPA's budget. The single factor in our analysis that correlates significantly with the EPA's budget trend over the period of our study is the outcome of General Social Survey polling on the public's environmental attitudes. The effect of this variable is sizable. The results of our analysis indicate that an increase (or decrease) of 10 percentage points in net public support for the environment compared to the previous year as measured using the General Social Survey data is associated on average with an increase (or decrease) of approximately 3.9 percentage points compared to the previous year for the EPA's budget.

There are two important caveats, however. First the relationship between changes in public attitudes and changes in the EPA's budget only accounts for about 13 percent of the budgetary variation, leaving much of the observed trend in the agency's fortunes unexplained. Second, the effect of changes in public opinion related to the environment on the agency's budget occurs with a lag time of three years, which is a longer lag time than might be expected.[33]

Political theory generally favors a one-year lag time or at most a two-year lag time for the relationship between changes in public opinion and changes in an agency's budget. That is, policymakers in Congress may be affected by public attitudes during the calendar year preceding the time they make budgetary decisions for the following fiscal year, leading to a lag effect of one year.[34] The president's budget request, submitted to Congress some months beforehand, may plausibly be affected during its early development by public opinion in the year before that, leading to a lag effect of two years.[35] A lag effect beyond two years seems unlikely. Yet, as indicated in Figure 5.4, a relationship appears when presenting together the EPA's budget data for a given year and the General Social Survey polling data from three years beforehand.

The top line in Figure 5.4 presents the inflation-adjusted EPA budget data from Figure 5.1, with values on the left axis. The middle and bottom

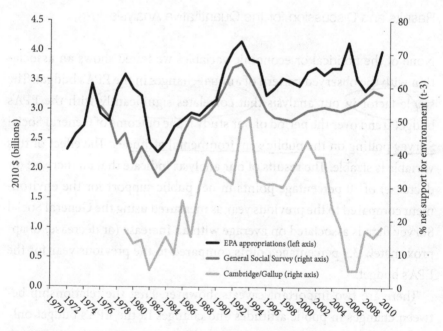

Figure 5.4 EPA Budget Data (Inflation-Adjusted) and Polling Data (Lagged Three Years).

DATA SOURCES: See footnotes 3, 29, and 30 for details. Dark (top) trend line shows budget data (values on left axis). Medium-shaded (middle) trend line shows General Social Survey data and light (bottom) trend line shows Cambridge and Gallup data (polling values on right axis).

lines present General Social Survey and Cambridge/Gallup polling data from Figure 5.2, lagged three years, with values on the right axis. As mentioned earlier, the two polling trends through 1998 are correlated with each other. Once lagged by three years, both are also correlated with the EPA budget trend line through 1998.[36] For the General Social Survey data, when lagged three years (though not for the Cambridge/Gallup data), the significance of the relationship with the EPA budget trend holds for the entire period of our study through 2010.[37] This observed correlation led us to include the General Social Survey data in our statistical analysis, with the data lagged by three years and converted to percent change from the prior year. As described at the beginning of this section, the outcomes of that analysis support the finding of a positive association between the General Social Survey data and the EPA's budget trend.

We hesitate to make strong claims for the results of our quantitative analysis, however. Our failure to find relationships between annual changes in the EPA's budget and the political and economic variables we tested does not confirm that such relationships do not exist. The relatively short time period of our study and the relatively large variation in the EPA's budget reduce the power of statistical techniques to reveal relationships among variables. Also, we find it hard to discern a plausible justification for a three-year lag time in the effect of public opinion on the agency's budget. It seems more likely in practice that the impact of current events would outweigh any residual effect on budgetary decision making of public opinion trends from three years beforehand. Despite these caveats, our findings could be interpreted as hinting at support for the incremental or issue-attention agency life cycle theories. We discuss next each possibility in turn.

The lack of any observable impact from political and economic changes over time suggests that agency budgets may be largely unaffected by external forces, as the incremental model implies. In addition, as described earlier, the annual change in the EPA's inflation-adjusted budget from 1973 to 2010 averaged a modest, superficially incremental, 1.9 percent increase. However, we believe this apparent support for incrementalism is ultimately not compelling. As we discuss further in the next section, the change in the EPA's budget from the previous year, positive or negative, was 15 percent or greater in eight out of the thirty-eight years studied. Frequent shifts of this magnitude do not accord with an incremental theory of agency life histories.

The case for the issue-attention model is somewhat stronger. The match in Figure 5.4 between the General Social Survey polling data with a lag time of three years and the EPA budget data is striking. The relationship holds in the results of our analysis. Moreover, as discussed above, the political history of the impacts of public environmental attitudes on Congress and presidents from the 1970s through the 1990s conform to expectations.

Yet several factors undermine this apparent support for the issue-attention model as well. First, as indicated in Figure 5.4, the strength of the relationship between the EPA's budget and public opinion depends on the phrasing of the question in surveys. The Cambridge/Gallup data focusing on the public's prioritization of the environment and the economy does not match as well with the EPA's budget trend as does the General Social Survey data. Second, a comparison of Figure 4.1 from Chapter 4 and Figure 5.4 shows that neither polling trend line matches the budget trajectory of the CEQ, another environmental agency that might be expected to feel effects from shifts in public opinion similar to those experienced by the EPA. Third, as mentioned earlier, a three-year time lag for the effect of public opinion on agency budgets does not seem plausible. In sum, the issue-attention model, particularly as it highlights the role of public attitudes, provides useful insights. Yet overall this model does not constitute a reliable tool for explaining budgetary trends for the agencies we studied.

HISTORICAL CASE STUDIES

In the previous section, we noted that the wide variation in the annual change in the EPA's budget tends to limit the power of the statistical analysis. In this section, we explore the sources of this wide variation by looking more closely at the fiscal years in which the change in the EPA's operating budget from the previous year, positive or negative, was 15 percent or greater: 1975, 1976, 1978, 1982, 1991, 1996, 2007, and 2010.[38]

To narrow our examination of these case-study years, we focus on the gap for each year between the president's budget request and the actual budgetary authority granted by Congress.[39] Then, to explore finer-grained differences in priorities between the president and Congress, we examine changes in the accounts within the annual budget. In examining the case-study years, we also consider the effects of party control in Congress and the White House during these years. Finally, at the end of the section, we discuss the increase of 11 percent in 2006, which is of interest because it reflects a large, unexplained, single-year spike in one account within the EPA's overall budget.

Overview of Presidential and Congressional Budgetary Support for the EPA

To prepare for the examination of the gap between presidential budgetary requests for the EPA and actual congressional budgetary authority granted to the agency in the case-study years, we first review the gap as it varied over the entire period of our study. Figure 5.5 presents the trends in

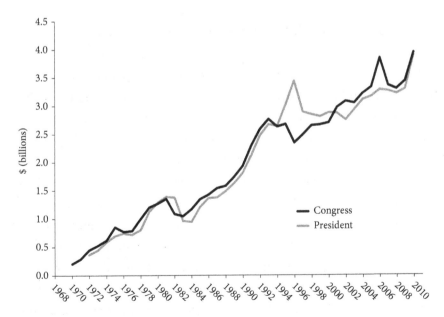

Figure 5.5 Presidential Budget Requests and Congressional Budget Authority Granted.
DATA SOURCE: See footnote 3 for details. Both congressional appropriations (darker trend line) and presidential requests (lighter trend line) are in nominal dollars.

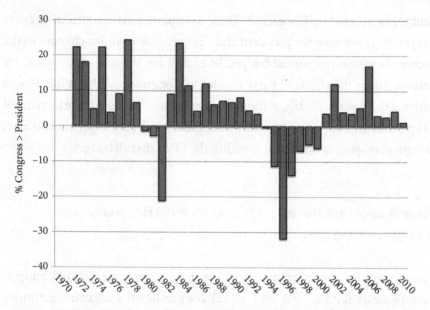

Figure 5.6 Percentage by Which the Budget Authority Granted by Congress Is Greater than (Bars Above Zero) or Less than (Bars Below Zero) the President's Budget Request.

DATA SOURCE: See footnote 3 for details.

nominal dollars. The lighter line represents presidential budgetary requests and the darker line represents congressional budgetary authority granted.

Figure 5.6 displays the gap in percentage terms. A bar extending above the zero line in Figure 5.6 indicates that Congress granted more funding for the EPA in that year than the president requested. A bar extending below the zero line indicates that Congress granted less funding for the EPA in that year than the president requested.

These two figures demonstrate that Congress has generally been more generous toward the EPA than presidents have been.[40] Bars extend above the zero line for twenty-nine of the thirty-nine years in Figure 5.6, and the darker line is above the lighter line in Figure 5.5 for a commensurate number of years. The presentation in percentage terms allows for clearer comparisons of the size of the gap over time. For example, the gaps illustrated in Figure 5.6 generally appear larger in the earlier years than they do in Figure 5.5, as compared to later years. This distortion results from the increasing size over time of the baseline budget in nominal dollars.

Several of the case-study years listed at the beginning of this section stand out in Figures 5.5 and 5.6 while others do not. Figure 5.6 highlights the striking gaps in 1982 and 1996, when Congress appeared to provide substantially less funding for the EPA than the presidents requested.[41] Figure 5.5 shows the spike in budget authority granted by Congress in 2006 compared to the president's request in that year. The case-study years that do not stand out in Figures 5.5 and 5.6 are those in which the president and Congress generally agreed on the cuts or increases in the EPA's budget.

A Comparison of Presidential and Congressional Budgetary Support for the EPA

Table 5.1 presents detailed information for the eight case-study years, those with changes in the EPA's budget of 15 percent or more, positive or negative, from the years immediately prior. For these years, the table summarizes presidential budgetary requests, congressional budgetary authority granted, and the difference between them, both by overall agency budget and by accounts within the budget.

Because in these cases we compare numbers within years rather than across years, the figures for the presidential budget requests and the budgetary authority granted by Congress are nominal, reflecting the actual amounts in the budget documents for those years. The left-hand column of the table identifies the fiscal year, the percent change from the previous fiscal year in inflation-adjusted budgetary authority (the case-study selection criterion), and party control of Congress and the White House in the prior calendar year when the budget for the fiscal year was determined.

Table 5.1 indicates that in three of the four years for which there were large budgetary increases compared to the previous year (1975, 1978, and 1991), Congress provided substantially higher budgetary authority than the presidents requested (22 percent higher in 1975, 24 percent higher in 1978, and 8 percent higher in 1991). Even in the fourth of these years with a large increase (2010), Congress was slightly more generous than the president (1 percent higher).

Table 5.1. Accounts within EPA Budget ($m): Proposed by President vs. Approved by Congress

Year	Account	President	Congress	% Difference
1975 (+26% from prior year)	Abatement & Control	408	437	7.1
	Research & Development	171	167	-2.7
	Energy Research & Development	0	134	n/a
	Agency & Regional Management	59	60	2.6
	Enforcement	53	51	-4.2
	Building & Facilities	0	2	n/a
	Total	695	850	22.3
1976 (−15%)	Abatement & Control	340	375	10.5
Ford (R)	Research & Development	163	265	62.4
House (D)	Energy Research & Development	112	0	-100
Senate (D)	Agency & Regional Management	66	72	9.0
	Enforcement	54	52	-3.0
	Building & Facilities	2	3	41.4
	Total	743	772	3.9
1978 (+18%)	Agency & Regional Management	72	83	15.2
Carter (D)	Research & Development	261	317	21.4
House (D)	Abatement & Control	395	521	32.0
Senate (D)	Enforcement	68	74	7.2
	Buildings & Facilities	1	0	-100
	Total	803	999	24.4

1982 (−24%)	Salaries & Expenses	646	555	−14.0
Reagan (R)	Research & Development	229	154	−32.7
House (D)	Abatement, Control, & Compliance	492	373	−24.2
Senate (R)	Buildings & Facilities	6	4	−45.5
	Total	1,376	1,086	−21.1
1991 (+18%)	Salaries & Expenses	1,000	994	−0.6
GHW Bush (R)	Research & Development	249	260	4.2
House (D)	Abatement, Control, & Compliance	865	979	13.1
Senate (D)	Buildings & Facilities	13	40	207.7
	Total	2,127	2,300	8.1
1996 (−15%)	Program & Research Operations	1,042	0	−100
Clinton (D)	Research & Development	477	0	−100
House (R)	Science & Technology	0	540	n/a
Senate (R)	Buildings & Facilities	113	110	−2.5
	Abatement, Control, & Compliance	1,809	0	−100
	Environmental Programs & Management	0	1,697	n/a
	Total	3,441	2,347	−31.8

continued

Table 5.1. (CONTINUED)

Year	Account	President	Congress	% Difference
2007 (−15%)				
GW Bush (R)	Science & Technology	834	769	−7.8
	Environmental Programs & Mgt.	2,392	2,554	6.8
House (R)	Buildings & Facilities	40	40	0
Senate (R)	Total	3,266	3,363	3.0
2010 (+15%)	Science & Technology	842	881	4.6
Obama (D)	Environmental Programs & Mgt.	3,024	3,028	0.1
House (D)	Buildings & Facilities	37	37	0
Senate (D)	Total	3,903	3,946	1.1

SOURCE: Office of Management and Budget, *Budget of the United States Government*, FY 1972–2012, Federal Reserve Archives, http://fraser. stlouisfed.org/publication/?pid=54. See footnote 3 for additional details.

NOTES: Dollar values are nominal; totals may not reflect actual sums of values because of rounding and because some minor accounts are omitted from the table.

In two of the four years in which there were large budgetary decreases compared to the previous year (1976, 1982, 1996, and 2007), Congress acted to limit the size of the decrease by adding back some budgetary authority compared to the presidents' requests (4 percent more than requested by the president in 1976 and 3 percent more in 2007), although the budgetary authority granted in these years was still sharply lower than the prior years. In the other two years, the numbers indicate that Congress took the lead in driving the budget reduction (providing 21 percent less than the president's budget request in 1982 and 32 percent less in 1996). As we describe below, however, the figures for 1982 do not present an accurate picture. In that year, the Reagan administration in its first budgetary cycle coordinated with congressional allies to reduce the EPA's budget through a legislative mechanism. Thus it appears that Congress initiated the cut when the impetus came from the White House.

For six of the eight case-study years with changes in the EPA's budget from the prior year of 15 percent or greater, Congress was more generous toward the agency than was the president. This matches the overall pattern revealed in Figures 5.4 and 5.5. Congress has given the EPA a higher budget than that proposed by the president in about three quarters of the years from the agency's establishment through 2010, and this trend has held in the years of highest budgetary volatility as well.

The President, Congress, and the Accounts
Within the Annual Budgets

The data in Table 5.1 also reveal differing priorities for the president and Congress beyond disagreements over the agency's total budget in many of the case-study years. For example, Congress in 1975 substantially increased budgetary authority for the core function of pollution abatement and control. In that year, Congress also created a new account titled Energy Research and Development and provided funding not requested by the president. In 1976, in a turnabout, the president requested money for the Energy Research and Development account but Congress eliminated it, possibly in anticipation of the creation of the Department of Energy, which occurred in 1977. However, Congress in 1976 did allocate substantially more funding than requested by the president for research and development. In 1991, Congress chose to provide three times as much as the president requested for buildings and facilities. In 1996, Congress not only cut the agency's overall budget but also significantly reconfigured the accounts within the budget.

The frequent shifts described in this section reflect ongoing tensions between the priorities of presidents and Congress. These changes in accounts within the annual budget have destabilizing effects on the agency independent of overall changes in the total budget.[42]

The Impact of Party Control on the EPA's Budget in the Case-Study Years

The data in Table 5.1 show that all four years of major budgetary increases for the EPA occurred when Democrats controlled both the House and Senate (1975, 1978, 1991, and 2010). Yet one of the years with a major decrease (1976) also occurred when Democrats controlled both houses of Congress, and one other year with a major decrease occurred when Democrats controlled the House of Representatives (1982). Two of the four years of major increases for the EPA's budget occurred under Republican presidents (1975 and 1991) and two occurred under Democratic presidents (1978 and 2010). Three of the four years of major decreases occurred under Republican presidents (1976, 1982, and 2007) and one under a Democratic president (1996). These inconsistent effects of party control in Congress and the White House help explain why our statistical analyses failed to find significant correlations between political variables and changes in the EPA's budget over the time period of our study.

Through the lens of political history, some of these results match expectations and some are unexpected. For example, the sharp reduction in the EPA's budget in fiscal year 1996 matches expectations. When Republicans in the 1994 midterm elections gained control of the House for the first time in forty years, they moved assertively to shrink government, with a particular focus on reducing environmental regulations. At the same time, however, President Clinton requested a sizable increase in the EPA's budget. Consequently, the data in Table 5.1 and Figure 5.6 show that Congress imposed its deepest cut compared to the president's request in 1996.

On the other hand, the figures for 1982 at first glance appear unexpected. The generally accepted narrative for the history of the EPA at this time is that President Reagan drove the sharp cuts in the agency's budget and that Congress attempted to push back against these reductions.[43] The data in Table 5.1 and Figure 5.6 for 1982 appear to conflict with this interpretation, as the budget authority granted by Congress in that year was more than 20 percent lower than the amount requested in the president's budget. As John William Ellwood reported at the time, however, the gap between the president and Congress for fiscal year 1982 is deceiving.[44]

Ellwood describes how "the Reagan administration and its congressional allies sought a legislative mechanism" to achieve the sharp cuts in federal domestic spending the president desired. Working with Republicans and conservative Democrats to circumvent the Democratic leadership in the House, the administration determined that the "reconciliation provisions of the Congressional Budget Act provided the solution. By putting all the cuts into a single bill, the advocates of reductions were able to obtain a single vote on the overall magnitude of the reduction rather than many votes on individual programs."[45] Thus, for fiscal year 1982, the Omnibus Budget Reconciliation Act of 1981 more accurately reflected President Reagan's wishes than did the president's budget. During the remainder of the Reagan administration, as indicated in Figures 5.5 and 5.6, Congress did consistently grant higher budgetary authority for the EPA than the president requested.

An Anomaly in 2006

Next we briefly discuss the gap for 2006 between the president's budget request and the congressional budget authority granted. Figure 5.5 shows a spike in the budget authorized by Congress in that year while the president's request followed the general pattern of the previous several years.

Our examination of accounts within that year's budget shows that the sharp one-year increase in 2006 was the consequence of a large and unexplained rise in "offsetting collections," defined as proceeds from "business-like transactions" involving the public or other government accounts.[46] In the case of the EPA, these collections may be fees, fines, user charges, and so forth. They are listed in the agency's budget under the Environmental Programs and Management account.

To give context, offsetting collections were $65 million in 2004, $209 million in 2005, $196 million in 2007, and $138 million in 2008. For 2006, however, the figure was $683 million, more than three times greater than any of the surrounding years.

As we were unable to find any explanation in publicly available documents for this spike, we contacted budget officials at the EPA. They confirmed our numbers and expressed surprise and interest in them. But after reviewing their records, they were also unable to explain the unexpected jump in offsetting collections for 2006.

Limitations of the Historical Case Studies

Our case studies of these years with large budgetary variations are necessarily exploratory, rather than explanatory. The overall patterns in Figures 5.5 and 5.6 and the differing priorities revealed in Table 5.1 raise questions about the strategies, tactics, and negotiating stances of presidents and legislators, and the political parties more generally, that these data alone do not allow us to answer. Next steps in research would include interviews and archival research to try to understand better the fine-grained politics behind the large budgetary changes in these years of high volatility.

Results and Discussion for the Historical Case Studies

In looking closely at annual budgets, we found that 74 percent of the time Congress provided more funding to the EPA than presidents requested.

A possible explanation is that Congress feels stronger ownership of and investment in the agency. Twenty committees in the Senate and twenty-eight in the House oversee the EPA's work. Although the agency often frustrates members of Congress, it remains a source of power and authority for many committee chairs and members.

We also observed substantial and disruptive year-on-year changes in accounts within the EPA's overall budget. Frequently Congress creates accounts, makes sizable changes to the funding for accounts, or eliminates accounts altogether. This may be a consequence of a congressional tendency noted by researchers to micromanage the agency.[47]

Also we discovered two anomalies. The first is the exceptionally large value of $683 million in offsetting collections in the 2006 budget, which as yet remains unexplained. The second is that, in apparent contradiction with the general understanding of scholars, the president proposed a higher level of funding for the EPA in 1982 than Congress enacted. This anomaly appears to be the result of a tactical collaboration between the administration and conservatives in Congress from both parties. Similar political tactics may lie behind other budgetary outcomes.

Overall the detailed case studies help us understand the general inability of the theoretical and empirical models we have considered to explain the movements in the EPA's budget over time. The case studies suggest that the processes for establishing the agency's budget are complex and idiosyncratic. Many political actors are involved, from Congress, the White House, the EPA itself, and concerned interest groups. Their motivations, incentives, and interactions are largely hidden from view, and their behaviors are likely influenced by many shifting, fine-grained contingencies that lead to unpredictable outcomes.

CONCLUSION

The large and irregular fluctuations in the EPA's budget resist systematic explanation. These substantial shifts have direct policy implications. Former EPA Administrator William Ruckelshaus, in his 1996 editorial entitled "Stopping the Pendulum," lamented that the exceptional volatility in the EPA's budget severely undermines the agency and hampers its effort to achieve its mission.

He wrote that "in the case of environmental policy these violent swings have had an unusually devastating—perhaps a uniquely devastating—effect on the executive agency entrusted to carry out whatever environmental policy the nation says it wants." He added, using a powerful metaphor, that "The EPA suffers from *battered agency* syndrome" (emphasis in original) and implored Congress and the public to "stop the continuous swings of political and rhetorical excess that have caused much of the damage."[48]

Ruckelshaus offered the following explanation for the violent swings in the agency's fortunes: "The anti-environmental push of the nineties is prompted by the pro-environmental excess of the late eighties, which was prompted by the anti-environmental excess of the early eighties, which was prompted by the pro-environmental excess of the seventies, which was prompted ... Why go on? The pattern is quite clear."[49]

Our research shows that this pattern is not as clear as it appears. The image of pendulum swings suggests regularity and predictability. However, the agency life cycle theories we considered generally do not provide a good qualitative fit to the trajectory of the EPA over the full time period our study, and our empirical analyses exploring the effects of political, economic, and social factors on the agency's budget failed to generate a convincing explanatory model. The swings in the EPA's budget constitute a powerful phenomenon with significant policy implications, but the reasons behind the phenomenon remain poorly understood.

In our work described in this chapter, we do not solve this puzzle, but we make some progress and help illuminate the dimensions of the problem. We show that the political and economic variables that might be expected to drive budgetary changes at federal agencies do not appear to be effective predictors in the case of the EPA. We uncover a correlation between public opinion and the EPA's budget, but only when the relevant question on surveys is asked in a particular way and only when including a lag time that is longer than theory appears to justify. Ruckelshaus, writing in 1996, sharply criticized Congress for its attacks on the EPA, but our research indicates that over the longer term presidents have been much more likely than Congress to push for reductions the agency's funding.

In Chapter 6 we review the efficacy of the theoretical agency life cycle models given our findings reported in Chapter 4 on the CEQ and in this chapter on the EPA. In Chapter 7, we consider possible futures for the two agencies over the next several decades under various scenarios. Given the uncertainties we have encountered in explaining past trends, we acknowledge that our projections for the future are educated guesses at best.

Comparing the Paths of the Council on Environmental Quality and the Environmental Protection Agency and Assessing the Life Cycle Models

In Chapters 4 and 5, we used four organizational life cycle models to develop predictions for the trajectories of the Council on Environmental Quality (CEQ) and the Environmental Protection Agency (EPA)'s appropriations over the forty-year period from their births in 1970 through 2010. In this chapter, we review findings from our studies of the CEQ and EPA, and we offer a general assessment of the power of the theoretical agency life cycle models. We also employ a framework we developed for comparing the models and for classifying the key variables in those models. This framework provides a means to move beyond the constraints of the existing literature, in which life cycle models are placed in either the "internalist" or "externalist" camps.

FRAMING THE STUDY OF THE CEQ AND EPA LIFE HISTORIES

We framed our study of the CEQ and EPA with two general views of what happens to public organizations during the process of implementing public law. One view is that the life of the executive branch organization will be relatively stable and untroubled as its leaders and professional staff pursue the organization's statutorily assigned mission. The underlying presumption here is that all of the important political questions related to the tasks assigned to the agency have been addressed in the public law itself. Consequently, the work of the agencies will be largely technical and uncontroversial.

The alternative view is that the political struggle over the passage of the laws the agencies are supposed to implement continues during the implementation stage of the policymaking process. The supporters of the law, inside and outside government, support the agency and its efforts. The opponents of the law, however, not only oppose the agency but also attempt to derail, or at least delay implementation of, the law. Thus, an agency's trajectory over time, in the form of its resources for and vigor in support of its assigned implementation tasks, will depend in large part on the balance of power, inside and outside government, between those who support and oppose the agency.

While these two perspectives provide a useful starting point for examining what happens to an executive branch agency after its birth, the four theoretical agency life cycle models we employed in this study, the biological, partisan political, incremental, and issue-attention models, offer a fuller range of perspectives on what might happen to an agency, and especially an agency's resources, over time. Specifically, using these four life cycle models, we developed rough qualitative predictions about the paths we might expect to see for an agency.

The schematic presentations of predictions generated from the models were presented in Chapter 3. The schematic presentations show four (very) different predicted life cycle paths, because each of these models is built upon different variables that (are expected to) drive growth and decline in the agency's budgetary resources.

It has become common practice in the academic literature to divide these four life cycle models into two groups: internalist and externalist. The incremental model is the only one of the four that clearly fits within the internalist grouping. Yet, as we pointed out in Chapter 3, a variable classified in one of the four models as an "internal" variable might be classified as an "external" or "exogenous" variable in another model. This confusion in the way variables are labeled makes comparisons of the relative predictive and explanatory power of the models especially challenging.

REVIEW OF FINDINGS ABOUT THE LIFE CYCLES OF THE CEQ AND EPA

The most important conclusion we can draw from our study of the life histories of the CEQ and the EPA is that their trajectories were neither smooth nor predictable. Both of these executive branch organizations were frequently, and sometimes dramatically, affected by the actions of elected officials in the U.S. government. The actions taken by those elected officials appeared to be driven by a variety of factors, some of which operated within and some of which operated outside the governmental system.

The volatility in the life cycles of the CEQ and EPA can be highlighted by the large swings that occurred in their appropriations. Specifically, on six different occasions between 1970 and 2010, increases or decreases of more than 50 percent occurred in the CEQ's annual appropriations. Swings of 25 percent or more occurred in the CEQ's annual appropriations nine times. Likewise, increases of 15 percent or more occurred in the EPA's annual appropriations on eight different occasions, even though its base budget was much larger than the CEQ's.

In the case of the CEQ's appropriations, the largest cut in dollar terms was the result of reductions the Reagan administration initiated in the Omnibus Reconciliation Act of 1981.[1] The largest cut in percentage terms occurred during the Clinton administration in 1994, when President Clinton wanted to fold the CEQ into the EPA and make the EPA a cabinet department.

The largest reduction in the EPA's funding, in both absolute and percentage terms, occurred in 1982 as part of the Reagan administration's budgetary initiatives in the Omnibus Reconciliation Act of 1981.

We also discovered that, while the CEQ and EPA had a s
function, there were important differences in the life cycle t:
the two organizations.

The most important difference was that three different presidents,
Carter, Reagan, and Clinton, considered terminating the CEQ or merg-
ing it into the EPA. In contrast, no president proposed elimination of the
EPA over the forty-year period from 1970 to 2010.

The primary motivations of the three presidents who considered terminating or merging the CEQ differed. The motivation for Presidents Carter
and Clinton was primarily administrative. In both cases, a desire to re-
organize the Executive Office of the President was an important factor.[2]
President Reagan's motivation, however, was ideological; he was opposed
to environmental regulation.

A second key difference between the life cycle trajectories of the CEQ
and EPA is what happened in the aftermath of the Reagan budget cuts in
FY 1982. The CEQ's appropriations never returned to the levels reached
prior to President Reagan's deep cuts.

In contrast, resource allocations for the EPA began to move in a positive direction in FY 1984, only two years after Reagan's cuts. As the data
in Figure 5.3 show, however, Congress, rather than the president, was
driving the growth in the EPA's resources between 1984 and 1988. Congress continued to increase the EPA's resources between 1989 and 1992.

FINDINGS ABOUT THE AGENCY LIFE CYCLE MODELS

Our general conclusion about the four life cycle models employed in our
study is that none of them can serve as a "grand theory" of what will
happen to an executive branch agency during its life cycle. This conclusion
is based on our empirical research, in which we discovered that the actual
trajectories or paths of the CEQ and EPA did not fit the predictions developed from any of the four models over the full forty years of this study.

While this conclusion might seem disappointing to scholars looking
for a single theory—or at least a dominant theory—of agency life cycles,

our conclusion is not unique and perhaps should not be considered surprising. Theories of agency life cycles are but one class of organization theories. While a wide range of organization theories exist, even James Q. Wilson, one of the best and brightest contributors to the public administration literature, publicly expressed "grave doubts that anything worth calling 'organization theory' will ever exist."[3] Wilson came to this conclusion, even though he acknowledged that, as a young scholar, he hoped he would be able to set forth "a simple, elegant, and comprehensive theory."[4]

It is also important to note, however, that, even though we did not find a single organization life cycle theory that fit the paths of the CEQ and EPA between 1970 and 2010, we did find that each of the four models employed in our study could be used to explain at least some elements of what happened to both agencies during particular segments of the forty-year period.

In this regard, our findings correspond, at least in part, to James Q. Wilson's conclusion: "Theories will exist, but they will usually be so abstract or general as to explain rather little. Interesting explanations will exist, some even supported with facts, but these will be partial, place- and time-bound insights."[5]

Wilson's insight also provides a way to put a key finding from our research into perspective. We found that the issue-attention model was the best-performing model in our study over the forty-year period for both the CEQ and EPA. For almost half of the time period between 1970 and 2010, the appropriations path, and especially the changes in the direction of that path, for both organizations could be explained, at least in part, by employing the issue-attention model. Furthermore, the predictions generated from the issue-attention model with respect to appropriations often fit the actual appropriations path of the agencies during those segments of time.

Why was the issue-attention model the best-performing model in terms of capturing the overall pattern of the rise and decline in the resources of the CEQ and EPA? The core premises of this model are more contingent and time-bound than the other three models. A "social issue," such as ecology, rises to prominence in the media and public attention, and the public demands that legislators fix the problem. Then, as Anthony

Downs predicted, the difficulty and costs associated with fixing the problem become known, the issue starts to fade, and it is replaced by a new issue.[6] Yet, for a variety of reasons, including new discoveries and new disasters or crises, an "old" issue, like ecology, will rise again on the public agenda and on the legislative agenda.

For example, we found that the issue-attention life cycle model served as a very useful tool for predicting and explaining the creation and rapid increase in the resources of the CEQ and EPA during the first half of the 1970s. We also found that the issue-attention model provides a means to explain, at least in part, the key segments of the growth and decline in the two agencies' resources over the full forty years between 1970 and 2010. That rise and decline appears to roughly approximate the rise and decline in the intensity of public interest, and thus legislators' interest, in environmental problems.

In addition to assessing the performance or value of the models on the basis of the frequency with which they served as useful vehicles for explaining the ongoing rise and decline of appropriations, we can also make judgments about relative value on the basis of whether a model fit what happened during a pivotal segment of time in the life cycle of the CEQ or EPA. In this regard, we found that the partisan political model was the best-performing model.

Specifically, we found that the partisan political model fit or captured what turned out to be the defining moment in the CEQ's life cycle. President Reagan was ideologically opposed to the CEQ's social function. Since Congress would not support his goal of terminating the CEQ, the president decided to defund the organization in the Omnibus Reconciliation Act of 1981. In this manner, and by appointing a loyalist to chair the CEQ, President Reagan and his senior advisors put the CEQ into the equivalent of a deep slumber.

President Reagan was also ideologically opposed to the EPA's social function, and he made deep cuts in its budget as part of the Omnibus Reconciliation Act of 1981. The 25 percent cut in the agency's 1982 budget authority damaged, but did not permanently reset, the agency's life cycle trajectory. Congress began increasing the agency's appropriations again in 1984.

The initial report of our findings about the time segments in which one of the models seemed to fit what actually happened, or at least provides a basis for explaining what happened, to the CEQ and the EPA is provided in Table 6.1. Table 6.1 provides a useful representation of the time segments in which our two best-performing models, the issue-attention and the partisan political models, seem to fit. Yet, two important features of the information presented in the table deserve additional attention. First, neither the biological model nor the incremental model appears in the table. Second, there are some blank spaces in the columns for the CEQ in Table 6.1. Both of these gaps will be discussed below.

The Incremental and Biological Models

As a quick scan of the entries in Table 6.1 shows, none of the life cycle models has been placed in the part of the table for the CEQ during George W. Bush's first term (2001–2004). The basic explanation for this gap is that, contrary to the predictions generated from the partisan political model, the CEQ's appropriations did not drop during that period. In fact, appropriations were relatively stable for the 2002–2005 budget years.

Given this circumstance, the incremental model could be placed in this time segment. Yet, as reported in Chapter 4, the incremental model does not provide a useful explanation for this apparent stability. The CEQ was not living in "a world of its own," and it was not being buffered or protected by a relatively closed decision-making process controlled by the agency, the Office of Management and Budget (OMB), the appropriations committees, and friendly interest groups. President Bush and his key advisors were setting the CEQ's appropriations.

Under Chairman James Connaughton, the CEQ was reenergized, and it was being led in a manner that fit the president's strong ideological objections to environmental regulation. That is to say, the CEQ's mission and statutory duties were "reinterpreted" to fit the president's antiregulatory ideology.

Table 6.1. **LIFE CYCLE MODELS THAT FIT AND/OR EXPLAIN THE CEQ AND EPA TRAJECTORIES**

Fiscal Year	CEQ	EPA
1970–71	Issue-attention model: Ecology	Issue-attention model: Ecology
1972–73	Issue-attention model: Ecology	Issue-attention model: Ecology
1974–75	Issue-attention model: OPEC oil embargo & recession	Issue-attention model: OPEC oil embargo & recession
1976–77		Issue-attention model: Ecology
1978–79	Issue-attention model: Iranian hostage crisis	Issue-attention model: Iranian hostage crisis
1980–81	Partisan political model: Reagan Issue-attention model: Recession	Partisan political model: Reagan Issue-attention model: Recession
1982–83	Partisan political model: Reagan	Issue-attention model: Congress
1984–85	Partisan political model: Reagan	Issue-attention model: Congress
1986–87	Partisan political model: Reagan	Issue-attention model: Congress
1988–89	Issue-attention model: Ecology	
1990–91	Issue-attention model: Ecology	
1992–93	Issue-attention model: Ecology	Issue-attention model: Ecology
1994–95		Partisan political model: Gingrich et al.
1996–97	Partisan political model: Clinton	
1998–99	Issue-attention model: Ecology	
2000–01	Issue-attention model: Ecology	Issue-attention model: Ecology Partisan political model: G.W. Bush
2002–03		Partisan political model: G.W. Bush
2004–05		Partisan political model: G.W. Bush
2006–07	Partisan political model: G.W. Bush	Partisan political model: G.W. Bush
2008–09	Issue-attention model: Ecology	Issue-attention model: Ecology
2010–11	Issue-attention model: Ecology	Issue-attention model: Ecology

2011–2016
2017–2021

Even though Connaughton was a lawyer, he explicitly said in an interview that his job was to serve the president and do what the president wanted him to do.[7] So, despite the clear instructions in the National Environmental Policy Act (NEPA) that the CEQ and its chair serve as the lead entity for coordinating efforts to protect human health and the environment, the CEQ was used to slow, modify, block, or overturn provisions in statutory law and administrative rules.

It is also worth noting that during President George W. Bush's second term, the CEQ's appropriations path did fit what we predicted on the basis of the partisan political model. A substantial cut (20 percent) was made in the CEQ's appropriations in 2006, followed by smaller cuts in 2007 and 2008. Even with a smaller resource base, however, under Connaughton's leadership the CEQ continued to be an energized agency that played the role President Bush wanted it to play—regardless of the statutory assignments clearly articulated in NEPA.

Another way in which the picture presented in Table 6.1 can be enhanced or expanded is to report on the ways in which the biological model can be used to explain what happened to the CEQ during particular segments of time. For example, the predictions developed on the basis of the biological model fit the actual appropriations for the CEQ during its first four years, when its resources grew rapidly and it appeared to pass through what Anthony Downs calls the "initial survival threshold."[8]

In addition, the biological model serves as a useful tool for explaining the CEQ's rapid growth in its early years and its passage through the critical survival threshold. In the biological model, as Downs articulated it, an energetic leader who is strongly committed to the agency's social function can be the single most important factor in its growth and survival.[9] Specifically, that leader must ensure that the agency performs effectively, and that leader must cultivate the support of interest groups and legislators in order to secure the funding necessary for its growth and survival. Russell Train was the CEQ's first chair, and his remarkable performance was a key factor in the CEQ's rapid growth.

The biological life cycle model can also be used to explain why the paths of the CEQ and EPA diverged so dramatically during the early

1980s under Ronald Reagan and during the mid-1990s under Bill Clinton. In his articulation of the key factors in the biological model, Downs says that size may be the most important factor in determining whether an agency survives over time.[10]

The CEQ was designed to be a small agency, with a few dozen employees. Thus it was vulnerable even after it appeared to pass through what Downs calls the "initial survival threshold." The EPA was born as a large agency, with more than six thousand employees. Furthermore, as it was given new pollution control responsibilities in statutory law, the EPA's size nearly doubled over time. Thus, its large size served as a key source of its protection.

In addition to size, there are two other factors that appear to be very important in the divergent paths of the CEQ and EPA, especially during the 1980s and 1990s. These factors could be defined as "internal" or agency variables, but they are not included in any of the four models we employed in our study. The two factors are the type of agency and the location of the agency.

When Congress created the CEQ in 1969, it placed the new agency in the Executive Office of the President. This proximity to the president and the president's key advisors can be an extraordinary asset in cases where the president, in this case Nixon, understands the role of the agency and appoints a person to lead the agency who is well known and respected by both the president and his advisors. In the early years of the CEQ's existence, perhaps even for the first decade of its existence, the agency benefited from this close proximity to the White House.

On the other hand, the CEQ's location in the Executive Office of the President put the agency at risk during Ronald Reagan's entire presidency and during the first two years of Bill Clinton's presidency. President Reagan tried to terminate the CEQ because he was opposed to its social function. President Clinton supported environmental regulation, but he tried to terminate the CEQ because he apparently did not understand the critical role the CEQ played in the development of environmental policy and the coordination of policy-implementation efforts across the executive branch.

In historical terms, Congress usually defers to the president's preferences with respect to the funding for, and even survival of, agencies in the
Executive Office of the President. In the case of the CEQ, the agency survived the efforts Reagan and Clinton made to terminate it only because
Congress did not support termination.[11]

On the other hand, Congress did accept Reagan's deep cuts to the agency's funding and the ongoing starvation of the agency during his eight
years in office. Congress also accepted Clinton's deep cuts to the agency in
1994. President Clinton moved to restore the agency's funding, however,
after Congress refused to terminate the CEQ.

A FRAMEWORK FOR COMPARING AND ASSESSING THE LIFE CYCLE MODELS

In the previous sections, we highlighted the ways in which the issue-
attention, partisan political, and biological models fit, or partially fit,
what actually happened to the CEQ and EPA over their life cycles between 1970 and 2010. Among the surprising findings of our investigation was that the fit between the incremental model and the actual
trajectories of the CEQ and EPA was relatively weak in comparison to
the other models.

Specifically, using the incremental model, we predicted that the CEQ
and EPA's appropriations would be relatively stable, with an upward trend
over the forty-year period we were examining. Furthermore, only small
increases in or decreases to the existing budgetary base were predicted.
The key explanation for this incremental path is that an executive branch
agency's appropriations are determined by negotiations between four entities: the agency, the OMB, the Congressional appropriations committees, and (friendly) interest groups.

In other words, a key presumption of the incremental model is that
the agency's appropriations are protected or buffered from forces outside
by this relatively closed and cozy set of relationships. Indeed, as we reported in the previous chapter, some scholars have, on the basis of the

[margin handwritten notes: "Not incre- mental" and "Incre- mental effectd"]

incremental model, suggested that the executive branch agencies seem to "live in a world of their own."[12]

Yet, the most interesting and important finding of our study of the life cycles of the CEQ and EPA is that the agencies' appropriations were very volatile between 1970 and 2010, with large increases and large decreases in annual appropriations occurring with surprising frequency. This finding stands in sharp contrast to the predictions we generated from the incremental model.

In short, on the basis of our investigation, we found that forces outside the "closed" system assumed in the incremental model frequently broke through the protective buffer. For example, President Reagan's effort to terminate and defund the CEQ resulted in a 75 percent reduction in the CEQ's 1982 appropriations. Additionally, President Clinton's efforts to terminate the CEQ and merge its functions into a newly designed cabinet department on the environment resulted in an 86 percent reduction in a base already diminished by the Reagan budget cuts.

Finally, it is worth noting that in some cases Congress limited the size of cuts presidents attempted to make in the CEQ and EPA budgets. In other cases, however, such as during Newt Gingrich's tenure as Speaker of the House, Congress was the key driver of decreases in the CEQ and EPA's appropriations.

In short, our study highlights the power that presidents and members of Congress have in the U.S. governmental system to enhance or diminish an executive branch agency's ability to implement statutory law. Our study also highlights the ways in which Congress can check the power of a president and the way in which a president can check the powers of Congress in the appropriations process.

Our study also highlights the fact that actions taken by various presidents and by members of Congress are often stimulated by factors or circumstances outside the basic institutions of the U.S. governmental system. These factors include economic recession, events and crises covered by the media, the rapid rise of new social problems on the issue agenda, foreign-policy problems, the rise of new interest groups, and elections.

Yet, the core presumption of the incremental model is that "internal" variables, not "external" variables, are the key to an agency's appropriations. Given this circumstance, and given the substantial differences we have reported in what is defined as an internal and an external variable in the four models we have employed in this study, we think it is useful to break out of the dichotomous classification scheme in the academic literature in which variables are classified as "internal" and "external."[13]

We think the way to break out of the constraint created by the existing classification scheme is to divide the variables that affect an agency's appropriations—and thus its life cycle—into the three key clusters: (1) agency-related factors, (2) governmental institutions and actors, and (3) factors outside government. We do so in Table 6.2. In this table, the key variables of the models, originally outlined in Table 3.1, are now sorted into three clusters. In our view, taking this action creates a revealing and important new picture of the similarities among and differences between the biological, partisan political, incremental, and issue-attention models.

Five important patterns can be identified by examining the way the key variables for each model are now sorted in Table 6.2. First, the full range of an executive branch agency's characteristics, including social function, leadership, growth/survival, size, performance, and age, appear to be central in only one model—the biological model. On the other hand, the social function of the agency is viewed as a key factor in the level of appropriations an agency gets in three of the four models: biological, partisan political, and issue-attention. The incremental model is the exception.

Second, the cluster of variables labeled "governmental institutions and actors" includes the president and Congress. In the biological, incremental, and issue-attention models (only) Congress is a key variable, while both the president and Congress are important variables in the political model. We found that presidents can have a powerful impact on an agency's budget, particularly if that agency has a social mission that a president finds objectionable. We also found that Congress can and sometimes does limit or check the impact a president might have on an agency's funding. Additionally, we found that Congress

Table 6.2. **FRAMEWORK FOR COMPARING LIFE CYCLE MODELS**

Key Variables	Biological	Partisan Political	Incremental	Issue-Attention
Executive Branch Agency				
Social Function	x	x		x
Leadership	x	x	x	
Growth/Survival	x			
Size	x			
Performance	x			
Age	x			
Type of Agency				
Governmental Institutions & Actors				
Executive Branch				
President		x		
Office of Mgt. & Budget			x	
Functional Rivals	x			
Allocational Rivals	x			
Congress	x	x		x
Appropriations Comm.			x	
Outside Government				
Elections		x		
Interest Groups	x	x	x	x
Economy				
Events/Disasters				x
Media Coverage				x
Social Problems				x
Cost of Solving Probs.				x
Dist. of Benefits & Burdens				x

can have a substantial independent impact on an agency's appropriations, in terms of both reducing and increasing the levels of funding requested by a president.

Third, key factors that exist outside government are included in all four models, but they make up the dominant cluster in only one model—the issue-attention model.[14] In the issue-attention model, factors outside government are viewed as the driver of actions taken by elected officials in the government. Yet, elections and the economy, two of the key variables we identified in our study as having an impact on budgetary decision making, are not explicitly identified by Anthony Downs as key causal variables in the issue-attention model.

Fourth, elections are identified as an important variable in only one model—the partisan political model. This might be surprising to political scientists who study elections, or to democratic theorists who identify elections as a key part of a democratic system. In our qualitative study of the CEQ and EPA, we highlighted the powerful effects that elections can have on the party and ideology of the person in the White House, and we showed the powerful effects that presidents of both parties can have on the size and frequency of changes in an executive branch agency's appropriations.

Fifth, interest groups are identified as a key factor in shaping an agency's appropriations in all four models. Yet, the challenges associated with defining all of the four key variables in the incremental model as "internal" variables are plain to see in Table 6.2. For example, interest groups are formed and exist outside the governmental system. Even though the representatives or members of interest groups have access to elected officials and their staff, interest groups are not a formal part of the institutions of government, and those interest groups do not have formal roles or responsibilities within the governmental system.

In sum, the framework we have developed and presented in Table 6.2 provides a useful way for comparing the key variables in each of the models. The framework also provides a systematic way to highlight some of our key findings. We also believe that this framework can be used as a tool for organizing future studies of the life cycles of executive branch agencies.

HIGHLIGHTING AND QUALIFYING THE FINDINGS
ABOUT THE CEQ, EPA, AND LIFE CYCLE MODELS

In this study of the life cycles of the CEQ and EPA, our primary goal has been to identify the key factors or variables that seem to affect, shape, or determine the agencies' resources over time. We have used appropriations as a proxy for agency vigor, or the energy the agency has in implementing public law. The key finding of our study is that the budgets of both the CEQ and EPA were highly volatile over the forty-year period from 1970 to 2010.

This finding is contrary to the incremental model, which most scholars accept as the best model for describing and explaining the appropriations of executive branch agencies. We also want to note that this volatility in the appropriations of the CEQ and EPA makes effective management and effective implementation of statutory law very difficult.

There are, however, a number of important limitations associated with this study that we want to acknowledge before we move on to Chapter 7, in which we attempt to make predictions about the future of the CEQ and EPA. First, our study has focused on only two executive branch agencies of the U.S. government. Thus, we cannot use the findings of this study to make general statements about other executive branch departments and agencies.

Second, our study provides a macro-view of what happened to the CEQ and EPA, which is just one approach that can be employed in the study of executive branch agencies. Middle-range and micro-level studies of these agencies can be coupled with our study in order to provide a more comprehensive picture of what has happened to these two organizations over time.

Third, we have taken the standard academic approach to the study of agency budgets or resources, which is to focus on inflation-adjusted figures. Governmental decision makers, including the president, the director and staff of OMB, and the members of the budget and appropriations committees of Congress may focus, in any given year, on the size of the proposed and actual changes in the base budget of an agency. Thus, the perspective of the decision makers might differ from the academic perspective.

Fourth, using the appropriations of an executive branch agency as a proxy for its vigor and its capacity to implement public law is only one approach that can be taken to describe and explain what happens to it over time. We recognize that a focus on other measures might yield different findings and conclusions. For example, federal courts have played a very important role in limiting the effect that NEPA, the CEQ, and the EPA have had on the other executive branch departments and agencies through the environmental impact statement process. Yet, no discussion of the courts and their impact is included in this study.

Finally, it is clear to us, as it has been to many other scholars, that the size and complexity of our governmental system, along with the size, complexity, and changing nature of the forces outside of government that operate on elected officials within that system, make effective description of what happens in government very difficult and explanation even more challenging. When description and explanation are so challenging, offering predictions about what will happen in the future, as we do in Chapter 7, is rather risky.

FUTURE RESEARCH ON THE LIFE CYCLES OF EXECUTIVE BRANCH AGENCIES

As noted in previous sections of this chapter, we developed a framework that can be used to systematically compare the four life cycle models we employed in our study of the CEQ and EPA. This framework can also be used to organize new empirical studies of other executive branch organizations. Among the benefits of employing the framework is that it includes all of the variables we identified in the four life cycle models employed in our study of the CEQ and the EPA, and it contains additional variables.

A number of approaches could be taken to extend our study of executive branch agencies. The findings of these studies would provide important information about whether, or to what extent, the life cycles of the CEQ and EPA are similar to or different from other executive branch organizations. *if similar size and location w/in Exec. Branch*

We found that the life cycles of the CEQ and EPA, which had shared social functions, were characterized by a high degree of volatility. At the same time, we found important differences in the life cycles of the two organizations. The small size of the CEQ and its location within the Executive Office of the President were key factors in those differences.

Given these findings, one approach that can be taken to expanding our knowledge of executive branch agencies' life cycles is to focus on the social function of individual organizations. So, a good starting point might be to look at executive branch organizations with functions that overlap those of the EPA's pollution control duties.

For example, the Department of the Interior's statutory assignments include protection of the national parks, wilderness areas, conservation areas for fish and wildlife, and oceans. By preserving healthy ecosystems in each of these key areas, the Department of the Interior also contributes to the filtering of human-generated pollutants, which, in turn, protects human health. Likewise, the statutory duties of the U.S. Forest Service, which is located in the Department of Agriculture, include protecting national forests. Healthy forests are natural filters of air pollutants and water pollutants and in this way protect human health.

It would also be possible to focus on organizations that have social functions that are different from the EPA's but, like the EPA, are "regulatory" agencies. The Securities and Exchange Commission, the Occupational Health and Safety Administration (in the Department of Labor), and the Food and Drug Administration (in the Department of Health and Human Services) might be good candidates.

A third option is to focus on organizations within the executive branch that are similar to the CEQ and EPA in size and type. In the case of the CEQ, similar types of organizations would be agencies within the Executive Office of the President. A study of the Council of Economic Advisors (CEA) might be a good place to start, particularly given the fact that the

CEQ was modeled after the CEA. In addition, the size of the CEA is similar to the size of the CEQ.

The size of an organization could also be an important factor in deciding what organizations are best suited for comparison to the EPA. In considering size, however, both appropriations and employment need to be considered.

For example, the Department of the Interior's appropriations are roughly the same size as EPA's, so the size is comparable on this measure. On the other hand, the Department of the Interior has more than five times the number of employees the EPA has.[15] The primary reason EPA's direct employment is smaller than Interior's is because EPA delegates most of its pollution control permitting functions, as well as the funds to support those functions, to the states. Thus, focusing on one of the major subunits of Interior, such as the National Park Service or the Fish and Wildlife Service, would yield a better comparison with EPA in terms of employment.

Similarly, selecting the Forest Service, rather than Department of Agriculture, might be a good choice for making comparisons to the EPA. The Department of Agriculture's appropriations are more than ten times the size of the EPA's, and it has more than seven times the number of employees.

In sum, conducting a life cycle study of an executive branch agency can be very challenging, but it can also be very rewarding. We believe the findings from our studies of the CEQ and the EPA make a useful contribution to our knowledge of what happens to executive branch organizations from their birth over multiple decades. We hope our work will stimulate additional studies of this kind.

The Future of the Council on Environmental Quality and the Environmental Protection Agency: 2015–2035

In this chapter, we consider possible futures for the Council on Environmental Quality (CEQ) and the Environmental Protection Agency (EPA) under several scenarios. Before beginning, we offer some caveats and disclaimers.

"Prediction is very difficult, especially about the future." This quotation—often credited to physicist Niels Bohr—captures the dilemma of prediction by stating it as a truism. Statistician Nate Silver, who won fame for accurately forecasting the 2008 and 2012 U.S. presidential elections, argues that in general the record of prognostication in public affairs, the field encompassing the ideas in this book, is particularly poor.[1] For example, in the late 1980s few specialists predicted the collapse of the Soviet Union, an event of enormous scale and importance that appears in hindsight to have been imminent and inevitable. More recently on the domestic front political experts generally failed to foresee the rise of the Tea Party, which has roiled the last three American electoral cycles and generated a significant rightward pull on the Republican Party and on U.S. politics more broadly.

Psychologist Phillip Tetlock, who examined the record of expert predictions in the arena of public affairs, reports poor results. In his research he found that "expertise . . . had no across-the-board effect on forecasting accuracy."[2] He observed that egregious prediction errors are surprisingly common, even among experts whose prediction skills are otherwise rated as better than average. About 10 percent of the time events actually occurred that these higher-performing experts had estimated to be impossible, while about 20 percent of the time events failed to occur that these experts had estimated to be sure things. The results were 10 percentage points worse in both directions for the poorer-performing experts in Tetlock's studies. Given these findings, the predictive limitations of the agency life cycle models we consider in this book are not surprising.

As discussed in Chapters 4 and 5, the qualitative models found in the literature and our statistical models are unable to capture all the ups and downs of the agencies' budgets over the past forty years. Our efforts to validate the models through "hindcasting"—that is, "predicting" observed historical trends given prior conditions—were at best only partially successful. Moreover, given the complexity and unpredictability of social systems, even if we had a validated model we could only guess at the appropriate political and economic parameters to enter for future years when attempting to predict the agencies' trajectories going forward.

A comparison of the hindcasting and forecasting powers in public affairs to those in climate-change science, another field that works in a challenging modeling environment, illustrates the limitations of the former. Climate-change models are now quite robust despite the inherent uncertainties in the systems they attempt to capture. Current climate models are successful in hindcasting trials over the past century within error ranges that are relatively well understood. Consequently climate modelers can now forecast with considerable confidence likely greenhouse-gas–emissions paths under various policy scenarios and the broad effects of these emissions trajectories on natural systems.[3] Modeling to predict political trends, such as in our area of federal-agency life histories, cannot compete with climate modeling in terms of accuracy or confidence. Political modeling generally has much less information to work with and must account for many more idiosyncratic contingencies.

Given the track record of predictions in the political arena, we are humble in this chapter in our forecasting for the CEQ and the EPA. The plausible future conditions we suggest are best considered thought exercises rather than definitive predictions.[4] First we briefly consider possible futures for the CEQ. We then focus on the EPA, beginning with what we believe to be low-probability scenarios falling at opposite ends of the political continuum of possible outcomes and then considering higher-probability scenarios that assume less dramatic changes in political conditions. We close the chapter with a brief discussion of possibilities for the overall direction of U.S. environmental policy over the next twenty years.

THE OUTLOOK FOR THE CEQ

The CEQ is a small agency. In some ways the hazards it faces are analogous to those observed in biology when assessing threats to the viability of small populations of organisms. Even without the emergence of major new risks, random reproductive or environmental fluctuations can drive small populations below the survival threshold. Similarly, small agencies are more susceptible than large agencies to elimination.[5] While abolishing a major regulatory agency like the EPA would be a rare, high-profile event, various minor contingences could potentially lead to the demise of a small agency like the CEQ.

Thus the likelihood of long-term survival for the CEQ may be lower than it is for the EPA, which we discuss in detail in the next section. As discussed in previous chapters, several sitting presidents have targeted the CEQ for elimination.[6] Presidents Carter and Clinton, who might have been expected to be friendly toward the agency, both considered merging it into the EPA as part of executive branch restructuring. Even when maintaining steady budgets for the CEQ, presidents, especially since 1980, have often marginalized the agency or used it for purposes other than its statutory social function.

The CEQ is in the Executive Office of the President, over which presidents normally have considerable discretion. In principle this would give a hostile president a relatively free hand to merge it into another agency or terminate it. However, Congress created the CEQ by statute as a key component of National Environmental Policy Act (NEPA), and so a president could not abolish it unilaterally. To date, Congress has declined to support any president's plan to do away with the agency.

Even though the CEQ has survived various threats to its existence over the past forty years, this is no guarantee of future longevity. Given the limitations of agency life cycle models, past history may be the best of an admittedly weak set of forecasting tools. Thus as a best guess we expect the CEQ to survive the next twenty years, as it has for the past forty years. We predict that some presidents will assign the agency important tasks and others will ignore it or redirect its efforts. The agency's budget and vitality will rise and fall with these presidential choices.

THE OUTLOOK FOR THE EPA

In discussing future prospects for the EPA, we begin by considering possible extreme outcomes. Imagine two opposing scenarios. In the first, a passionately antiregulatory president is elected with like-minded majorities in both houses of Congress. Among other priorities, the incoming president has promised to eliminate the EPA. Upon taking office, the new president and Congress terminate the agency. In the second scenario, a passionately "green" president is elected with like-minded congressional majorities. The incoming president has promised to make addressing climate change and promoting environmental sustainability the nation's top priorities. Upon taking office, the new president and Congress elevate the EPA to central status and provide funds to fully empower its activities. Here we consider the likelihood of either of these two scenarios coming to pass.

The End of the EPA?

In the nominating process leading up to the 2012 presidential election, the EPA was a frequent subject of scorn in Republican primaries. At an Iowa rally in 2011 Michelle Bachman said, "I guarantee you the EPA will have doors locked and lights turned off, and they will only be about conservation. It will be a new day and a new sheriff in Washington, DC."[7] Threatening rhetorical attacks on the EPA from the right have continued to the time of our writing of this chapter.[8] How likely is it that antiregulatory, Tea Party-inspired Republicans could secure the White House and both houses of Congress and eliminate the EPA?

For this scenario to be realized, a series of events would have to occur. First, a Tea Party activist or antiregulatory ideologue would have to win the Republican presidential nomination. Second, the nominee would have to win the general election. Third, the new president would have to take office with congressional majorities to support enactment of his or her policies. Fourth, the new administration, acting in concert with congressional leaders, would have to follow through on the promise to eliminate the EPA. Using recent political history, we estimate rough probabilities for these outcomes.

Beginning with the first postwar election of 1948, Republicans have eleven times gone through a nominating process not dominated by an incumbent Republican president standing for reelection. Only once has a candidate to the right of the party mainstream and without prior experience on the national stage won the nomination over the party favorite—Barry Goldwater over Nelson Rockefeller in 1964. Ronald Reagan helped pull his party to the right, but by the time he won the nomination in 1980, he had been part of three nomination cycles. He came close to winning the nomination over Gerald Ford in 1976. By 1980, he was no longer outside the party mainstream. Over the same time period, the Democrats have had fourteen open nomination cycles, and, similarly, a candidate to the left of the party mainstream has upset the party favorite only once—George McGovern over Edmund Muskie in 1972.

This suggests something on the order of a 10 percent chance of success for a far-right or far-left candidate seeking the presidential nomination in the two major American parties. Twenty-five nominating cycles constitute a small sample, however, and the right wing of American politics is currently highly influential. To avoid underestimating the likelihood of what otherwise may be an extreme outcome, we double the probability and estimate a 20 percent chance that a Tea Party-style Republican candidate will win the nomination in any given open nominating cycle over the next twenty years.

Given success in gaining the party nomination, how likely is it for an antiregulatory activist to win the general election? In the postwar period, no candidate significantly to the right (or left) of the party mainstream at the time of nomination has won the general election; both Goldwater and McGovern lost in landslides. Nevertheless, a candidate nominated by a major party clearly has a probability of winning the general election greater than zero. We estimate this conditional probability (the probability of a right-wing candidate winning the general election having won the Republican nomination) as something on the order of 45 percent.

How likely it is for a newly elected president to take office with his or her party in the majority in both houses of Congress? The only Republican president to do so in the postwar period was Eisenhower in 1952. However, Eisenhower lost control of both houses in the 1954 midterm election and never regained control of either house. George W. Bush did not take the presidency with majorities in both houses, but he achieved this mark at the midterm election of his first term and retained it for four years until the midterm election of his second term. For Democrats beginning in 1948, Truman, Kennedy, Johnson, Carter, Clinton, and Obama took office with majorities in both houses. Clinton and Obama, however, lost one or both houses at their first midterm election and never regained full control of Congress during their terms.

Overall since 1948, seven of eleven presidents elected for the first time came into office with their party in control of Congress. Six of these were Democrats, who were more likely to have the opportunity do so because their party controlled the House for forty years from the 1954 election to the 1994 election. Looking at congressional election cycles instead of presidential terms, there was unified government (with one party in control of the White House and both houses of Congress) for thirteen out of thirty-four of the two-year periods beginning with the 1948 election results. To be conservative (that is, to reduce the likelihood of failing to predict the EPA's demise), we estimate there may be a 60 percent chance that over the next twenty years a newly elected right-wing president would find like-minded majorities in control of both houses of Congress. As we discuss next, however, the probability that congressional leaders would eliminate a major agency like the EPA, even if a president of their own party requested the action, is lower, perhaps 20 percent at most.

There is an ongoing scholarly discussion about agency mortality rates. In a classic study, Herbert Kaufman examined agencies that already existed in 1923 or came into being over the fifty-year period from 1924 to 1973.[9] He found that 148 of the 175 organizations enumerated in his 1923 census were still in operation in 1973. This result indicates a long-term survival rate of about 85 percent, or, looked at another way, a death rate of less than 0.4 percent per year. Kaufman identified an additional 246 organizations that came into existence over the study period that survived until 1973. Thus Kaufman's work suggests a low overall mortality rate for government agencies.

Recently, researchers have updated and extended Kaufman's work. Carpenter and Lewis examined 398 government agencies that appeared between 1946 and 1997.[10] These scholars reported that 227, or about 57 percent, of the agencies they examined were defunct by the end of the study period. The median lifespan of the agencies studied was twelve years. Thus their findings suggest a high mortality rate for government agencies.

The different results can be explained in part by differences in the makeup of the datasets. Kaufman focused his study on agencies within cabinet departments and the Executive Office of the President. These agencies tend to be durable. Carpenter and Lewis, drawing their list from the *United States Government Manual*, examined a more diverse set of agencies in terms of size and function. Their more inclusive list captures organizations with a greater range of lifespans.

Carpenter and Lewis also followed Kaufman's lead in identifying variables that add to or reduce the threat to an agency's survival. According to their analysis, termination is less likely if the agency was created by statute or reorganization plan (as opposed to unilateral executive action), if the federal budget is in deficit (because agency termination has social and fiscal costs), and if political power in the federal government is divided (the hazard to an agency increases with political turnover, unified government, and hostile political leadership). According to this model, the way the EPA was created (by reorganization plan) and the existence of a budget deficit (near certain over the next twenty years) reduce the hazard to the agency's survival. The possibility in the current political climate of political turnover, unified government, and hostile political leadership adds to the hazard.

The size of the EPA and its responsibility for over twenty major laws passed by Congress favor its longevity, however. The elimination of large executive branch agencies or departments has been rare in U.S. history. In 1980, President Reagan took office with a powerful electoral mandate and the stated aim of doing away with the newly formed Department of Education. President Carter had signed the law creating the department in October 1979, and the agency had opened for business in May 1980. Ronald Reagan, on the campaign trail, immediately dubbed it "President Carter's new bureaucratic boondoggle" and promised to eliminate it if elected.[11] According to Downs's biological model, the department was vulnerable at this point, not yet having passed through the survival threshold. Yet it survived and even gained strength during President Reagan's first term. Concerns about poor educational outcomes in the United States became a political issue, and the president used the department to favor his priorities for promoting improved performance, including standardized testing, merit pay for teachers, and tuition tax credits for private schools.

Major government agencies have powerful vested interests, even among political leaders who might oppose their social functions. Congressional committees oversee the budgets and operations of federal agencies and derive power and authority from those activities. Twenty committees in the Senate and twenty-eight in the House have oversight responsibility for the EPA's work. This provides considerable inertia in favor of the organizational status quo. Large established agencies may suffer cyclical budgetary cutbacks and realignments of social function, but history indicates that they are far more likely to survive than not. Thus we suggest that even with an amenable Congress, a president seeking to terminate the EPA would likely have no better than a 20 percent chance of success.

Next we combine these conditional probabilities. We estimate a right-wing outsider has perhaps a 20 percent chance to win the Republican nomination, a 45 percent chance to win the general election given the nomination, a 60 percent chance of coming into office with congressional majorities in both houses given election to the presidency, and a 20 percent chance to succeed in eliminating the EPA given these prior outcomes. This gives an overall chance for the demise of the agency following an election cycle with an open nominating process for the Republican Party of less than one chance in fifty.[12]

The period of our twenty-year forecasting horizon includes the five presidential elections from 2016 to 2032. For both parties, 2016 is an open nomination cycle. Assuming conservatively that a Republican incumbent is standing for reelection only once before 2032, then Republicans will have four open nominating cycles. If the probability of the scenario leading to the elimination of the EPA is under 2 percent per open Republican election cycle, the probability of it happening over four election cycles is under 8 percent.[13] As discussed above, however, we have inflated the probability at each stage to reduce the likelihood of underestimating the outcome. Overall we conclude with moderate confidence that the elimination of the EPA is a low-probability event.

The Empowerment of the EPA?

End or Empowerment? Chances are about the same 1:50

The second extreme scenario, in which sometime over the next twenty years ideological, left-wing environmentalists succeed in securing the Democratic Party presidential nomination, winning a general election, and liberating the EPA from financial and political constraints, is also improbable. The pattern is similar to that described for the scenario leading to the elimination of the EPA. A candidate significantly to the left of the Democratic Party center is unlikely to come to power. It is also uncommon for agencies to be given anything approaching free rein for any extended period. After the attacks of September 11, 2001, intelligence, defense, and security agencies experienced substantial budgetary increases and considerably relaxed congressional and judicial oversight. The equivalent is much less likely for a domestic regulatory agency like the EPA.

More Likely Scenarios for the EPA

As with our discussion of low-probability outcomes, we use historical trends to point the way toward more likely futures for the EPA. Figure 7.1 shows the distribution of year-on-year budgetary changes from 1973 to

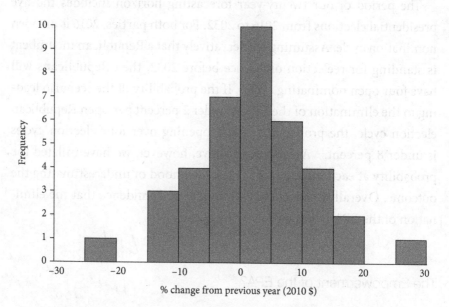

Figure 7.1 **EPA Budget 1973–2010, Distribution of Annual Percent Change from Previous Year (Inflation-Adjusted)**
NOTE: See Figure 5.3 for annual percent changes over time. As indicated in Chapter 5, footnote 20, the startup years of 1970–1972 are omitted.

2010. During this period, adjusting for inflation, the mean annual change in the EPA's budget was +1.9 percent, with a median value of +3.7 percent. For half the years (nineteen out of thirty-eight), the annual budget increased or decreased by 5 percent or less. As indicated by the standard deviation of 9.96, however, there were occasional wide fluctuations in other years. The agency has experienced eleven years with budgetary shifts from 6 to 12 percent, positive or negative, and six large swings of 15 to 18 percent. The most extreme cases were an increase of 26 percent (in 1975) and a decrease of 24 percent (in 1982). As we have discussed in previous chapters, this pattern does not fit with a common-sense use of the term "incremental." Even 5 percent annual shifts in budgets can be destabilizing for an agency, so double-digit changes surely entail disruptive realignments for staff and functions.

This history suggests a rough estimate of a 50 percent chance in any given year of a budgetary change of 5 percent or less, a 30 percent chance of a change on the order of 10 percent, a 15 percent chance of a major swing on the order of 15 percent, and a 5 percent chance of an extreme change on the order of 25 percent. We expect that the major swings when they come will follow from the internal and external contingencies described in Chapter 6, and will respond productively to retrospective explanation in those terms. Looking out twenty years, however, the timing of bureaucratic, political, economic, and social changes that may drive major shifts in the EPA's budgets are largely unpredictable.

While we cannot forecast specific events with confidence, there are two longer-term trends that may possibly lead to some modest average improvement in the EPA's fortunes between now and 2035. First, the Census Bureau forecasts that America will be a majority-minority nation by 2043, meaning that non-Hispanic whites will no longer constitute the majority of the population.[14] Low-tax, small-government, individualistic principles are traditionally less appealing to immigrants and minorities. Political analysts suggest that over the next two decades, the slow but steady demographic transition projected by the Census Bureau may favor Democrats while pressuring Republicans to adopt more centrist positions.[15] While the level of strong bipartisan support for environmental protection seen in the late 1960s and early 1970s is unlikely to reemerge over the next twenty years, incremental movement in that direction seems more likely to occur than not.

There are reasons to be confident that the demographic projections will hold. These large-scale structural trends are similar in strength to the trends incorporated in climate models for greenhouse-gas concentrations in the atmosphere. That is, there is already strong built-in momentum for the projected outcomes. The impacts of the demographic transformation are less certain, however. Immigrants and minorities do not form a homogenous voting bloc, and the political allegiances and policy preferences of these groups may change over time. Nevertheless, it seems more likely than not that the projected population changes will favor planks currently in the Democratic platform, including environmental protection.

Second, climate-change effects over the next twenty years are likely to become more apparent. Changes to weather patterns, water supplies, agricultural yields, suburban gardens, coastline stability, cooling bills, storm-damage costs, and so forth are likely to affect the general public more frequently. The increasingly noticeable effects of a changing climate may heighten environmental concerns. Over time, attacking pollution control regulations may become less likely to score political points on the campaign trail.

An increase in public support for environmental policies is less sure than the continuation of the movement toward a majority-minority electorate. Nevertheless, we suggest it is more likely than not that the combination of near-certain demographic changes and plausible changes in public attitudes resulting from observable effects of climate change may gradually convert the EPA from a political punching bag to more a respected agency thought by the public to deserve increased budgetary support.

THE FUTURE OF THE SOCIAL FUNCTION
OF ENVIRONMENTAL PROTECTION

The CEQ, although a small agency, plays an important role in the nation's environmental policymaking. The council's tasks include providing analysis and advice to the president, monitoring the implementation of the environmental impact statement process, coordinating matters related to the environment across the federal government, and proposing amendments or additions to the nation's suite of environmental laws.

The EPA, on the other hand, is a major line agency with responsibility for carrying out policies that have large-scale direct impacts on the environment and economy. The agency designs and implements regulations required under most of the environmental statutes enacted by Congress over the past forty years. Among other goals, these laws aim to improve the quality of the nation's air, water, and land; manage solid waste; and monitor hazardous and toxic substances. The EPA's changing fortunes over its history to some degree reflect the nation's fluctuating levels of commitment to environmental protection and satisfaction with the regulatory process. When elected leaders reduce the agency's budget, appoint hostile leadership, and limit its powers of regulation and enforcement, there may be costs in terms of public health and sustainability. Yet unnecessary social costs also arise when the laws are vague and unrealistic, or the regulations that follow from them are poorly designed and inefficient.

An important component of the story of environmental policy over the past forty years has been the effort to improve the regulatory process—that is, to ensure to the extent possible that the social benefits of regulations outweigh the social costs, that net social benefits are maximized, and that equity and fairness are accounted for. Between 1970 and the present, scientists have learned more about how human health and the environment may be harmed by the environmental side effects of economic activities. Similarly, policy analysts and economists over the past forty years have learned more about how regulations to address these adverse side effects can be reshaped to increase the social benefits and reduce the social costs of their implementation.

Many of the loudest attacks on the EPA voiced in the political realm are partisan, ideological, uninformed, or the result of private actors pursuing their own interests at public expense. However, these politically motivated criticisms can tap into broader background levels of dissatisfaction among those who pay the immediate costs of environmental protection, including firms, property owners, and consumers. The dissatisfaction of the affected public can arise from the real or perceived arbitrariness and wastefulness of regulations.

Policy analysts and economists assess inefficiencies and propose alternative approaches to make regulations more effective and less burdensome. While full coverage of the regulatory reform movement is beyond the scope of this book, we give a brief overview here because we believe the trend toward smarter environmental governance is a key part of the EPA's future in coming decades.

The environmental laws and regulations of the 1970s were essential first steps toward managing the nation's environmental concerns. In retrospect, however, given advances in economic and policy analysis, we can see that these laws did not account for the full complexity of the problems at hand. The Clean Air Act of 1970, for example, mandated air quality standards strict enough to protect even the most vulnerable members of society. Yet the law restricted cost accounting for ambient standards, thereby setting the stage for conflict over the standards, the science supporting the standards, and social priorities more broadly. The Clean Water Act of 1972 required that all discharges of pollution into surface waters be eliminated by 1985. This was an overly optimistic, unachievable deadline.

The laws of the 1970s incorporated a range of implicit assumptions subject to question in hindsight: that sufficient knowledge was available to understand and address environmental problems, that pollution should be cleaned up to a level that eliminated all harm regardless of cost, that polluters should bear the expense of the cleanup and that these costs would not ripple out into the larger economy, and that government agencies should prescribe, monitor, and enforce the mechanisms of environmental protection and could do so efficiently and effectively. These unrealistic assumptions led ultimately to continuing court battles as the EPA was caught between industry groups fighting against costly regulations and environmental groups demanding that the agency achieve mandated goals regardless of cost.

In implementing these laws, the EPA has typically used the regulatory approach of setting and enforcing standards—ambient standards, emissions standards, or, often, technology standards. In practice this strategy, sometimes labeled "command and control" or "rules and deterrence," is generally an inflexible mechanism.[16] As critics both inside and outside the EPA have pointed out, it tends to discourage innovation, foster an adversarial relationship between the regulator and the regulated, and overlook opportunities to achieve statutory environmental goals at lower social cost.

The rules-and-deterrence approach has produced important gains for the nation despite its inherent inefficiencies. This is especially true for improvements in air quality. Chapter 2 lists the progress made since 1980 in lowering airborne concentrations of lead, carbon monoxide, sulfur dioxide, nitrogen oxides, and ozone. Analysts generally agree that social benefits of achieving these gains have outweighed social costs by a wide margin.

The 1990 Clean Air Act Amendments required the EPA to assess efforts to improve air quality since the passage of the original Clean Air Act of 1970. In conducting this review, researchers estimated a minimum return on investment from air pollution control of ten to one, with far greater returns likely. The EPA's report estimated regulatory-compliance costs for the twenty-year period aggregated across the economy of about $500 billion, in 1990 dollars. The report estimated benefits to human health and other desired outcomes of between $6 trillion and $49 trillion, with a mean estimate of about $20 trillion.[17] The public-health benefits came primarily from the elimination of lead in gasoline and the reduction of hazardous particulates in the air. Studies suggest that the elimination of lead in gasoline alone had a net social benefit, in 1989 dollars, of approximately $200 billion per year in neurological and other harms avoided by the time the lead phase-out was completed in 1995.[18]

Economic theory and empirical analysis of trends in costs and benefits over time typically reveal a common pattern that each unit of additional environmental cleanup tends to have a higher incremental cost and a lower incremental benefit than the previous unit of cleanup. Sharply reducing air pollution compared to the weakly regulated period before 1970 was analogous to picking low-hanging fruit. Improving air quality generated high social benefits in terms of human health because most Americans lived in urban areas where the air was most polluted. The social cost of achieving these early gains was relatively low because the prior status quo included almost no effort to constrain emissions. Continuing efforts to make air quality standards more stringent, for particulates and ground-level ozone for example, are still likely to generate strong net social benefits even if the rules are less than ideally efficient and the net benefit per unit of pollution abated is on a declining path. Other regulations, such as those relating to the cleanup of hazardous waste sites, to give one example, may reach a point where costs outweigh benefits well before established standards are met. This is both because costs for this kind of remediation are high and because the adverse environmental and health effects are much more narrowly distributed than they are for air pollution.

The phase-out of lead in gasoline during the 1980s included components of a new regulatory approach that went beyond the standards-based strategy. Regulators distributed to refiners a limited supply of permits for lead in gasoline and reduced the number of permits over time. A market emerged in which refiners could bank or buy and sell these permits. This innovation allowed the transition away from leaded gasoline to occur at a lower total social cost. Firms able to lower their use of lead more cheaply had the incentive to do so. They could recoup their costs and even turn a profit by selling the permits they no longer needed to firms that could not reduce their use of lead as cheaply. Analysts estimated that this approach achieved lead-reduction goals at a cost that was several hundred million dollars lower than would have occurred under a mechanism imposing a single standard on all refiners.[19]

As we described in Chapter 2, the 1990 Clean Air Act Amendments applied a variation of this mechanism to the reduction of sulfur emissions from coal-fired power plants, also with notable success. Under the program regulators distributed a limited number of permits to emit sulfur dioxide but allowed regulated firms to buy and sell the permits, which were known as allowances. The total number of allowances set an overall limit on emissions. The market gave incentives for firms that could reduce emissions cheaply to take on the cost of doing so. It also gave firms incentives to develop new pollution reduction technologies. In effect firms with higher cleanup costs compensated the firms that reduced pollution by buying their excess allowances. Thus the social cost of reducing emissions to the level of the cap—that is, the overall cost that rippled out across the economy—was lower than it would have been under a scenario in which each firm had to meet the same pollution reduction standard. Analyses of the permit-trading program for sulfur dioxide emissions have found the environmental goals were achieved both more effectively (the Act's long-term goal was met by 2007 and substantially exceeded by 2010) and more cheaply (costs are estimated to have been 15 to 90 percent lower) than would have occurred under a standards-based regulatory regime.[20]

Following the success of the 1990 cap-and-trade policy for sulfur dioxide emissions, policymakers began to look for market-based or incentive-based mechanisms to address a wide range of environmental problems.[21] Along with cap-and-trade, the list of such strategies includes taxes on emissions, subsidies for renewable-energy development, public-disclosure requirements for hazardous wastes, and tradable quotas for sustainable management of natural resources such as fish stocks or irrigation water.

The influence of market-based responses to environmental dilemmas now reaches from the local to the global level. International efforts to address climate change from the Kyoto Protocol of 1997 forward have incorporated carbon-credit exchanges to reduce greenhouse-gas emissions. Under these policies, firms could earn carbon credits in various ways. For example, they could reduce emissions at their own plants, transfer clean technology to allow dirtier firms elsewhere to reduce emissions, or fund measures to reduce deforestation in areas that would otherwise be cleared, thus keeping carbon sequestered in trees rather released to the atmosphere. In 2007, the European Union implemented an emissions-trading program for greenhouse-gas emissions in all member countries. In 2008, nine adjacent states from New England and the Mid-Atlantic region of the United States (Connecticut, Delaware, Maine, Maryland,

Massachusetts, New Hampshire, New York, Rhode Island, and Vermont) formed the Regional Greenhouse Gas Initiative. Under this scheme, states auction allowances to regulated firms in the electricity-generation sector and use funds raised from the auctions to support initiatives to promote renewable energy and energy efficiency. In 2012, California established its own cap-and-trade program for greenhouse-gas emissions.

Most economists believe the most efficient way to achieve climate change mitigation goals is the imposition of a global carbon tax.[22] However, valuable second-best options include cap-and-trade, credit exchanges, offsets, renewable-energy subsidies, climate-friendly certification, and other incentive-based arrangements. As we write this chapter, the EPA has proposed regulations to address U.S. carbon emissions at the national level. Under the proposed regime, states will be assigned carbon-emissions limits, taking into account current usage patterns, and will be given flexibility in the ways they can meet the caps, including the use of credits, banking, trading, and other strategies. Even though greenhouse gases are not explicitly identified in the Clean Air Act, the Supreme Court has twice in recent years ruled that the EPA has the authority and responsibility to regulate these emissions and that the agency has considerable discretion in establishing the regulatory mechanisms to do so.

The EPA's primary approach in addressing most environmental problems remains a rules-and-deterrence approach. In many cases the relevant statutes make it difficult to explore other options. Moreover, while incentive-based policies are strongly supported by theory and have had some notable successes in practice, they often fail to live up to expectations.[23] For example, the Kyoto Protocol failed to slow growth in global atmospheric concentrations of greenhouse gases, and the European Union's emission-trading scheme has struggled to achieve its goals. Nevertheless, a key emphasis for the EPA as it moves forward will be to design regulatory approaches that are more efficient, effective, and equitable than traditional strategies.

Reducing pollution is rarely cost-free. The argument for undertaking environmental cleanup is that the benefits accruing to society will outweigh the costs. In introducing his administration's new greenhouse-gas regulations in 2014, President Obama acknowledged that they would likely raise energy prices. The president said, "People don't like gas prices going up; they are concerned about electricity prices going up . . . we've got to shape our strategies to address the very real and legitimate concerns of working families."[24] Ideally, regulations should be efficient, but also fair. They should account for inequities in the way costs are shared across society, and policy analysts and economists have found effective strategies for doing so in many cases.

Selling voters on new regulations that may adversely affect their household budgets is a challenge. The EPA's ideological and partisan adversaries can score political points by emphasizing the regulatory costs. As regulations become more flexible, fair, and efficient, and as the public becomes better educated about the associated benefits, voters may become less easily swayed by antiregulatory rhetoric in the environmental arena. Thus we believe that for reasons of economic efficiency and political feasibility the EPA will continue to move toward smarter regulations that achieve beneficial environmental goals more equitably and at lower cost.

CONCLUSION

To summarize our forecasts in this chapter, we expect the CEQ and the EPA to survive the next twenty years. However, these agencies, as they have for the past forty years, will continue to suffer occasional budgetary shocks, some severe. We expect that truly existential threats to the CEQ and the EPA, while of generally low probability, are more likely to emerge in the first decade of our twenty-year forecasting horizon than in later years. As time passes, we suggest that the significant demographic changes already under way, in conjunction with the possibility of rising awareness among voters of the adverse effects of climate change, may drive a modest swing back to the center in American environmental politics.

We argue that going forward, presidents and Congress should provide the CEQ and the EPA with budgets adequate for their tasks, and that these budgets should remain on reasonably steady trajectories in real terms, while accounting for increases in responsibilities. In Chapter 4, we reviewed recommendations included in a 2008 report from an eminent group of former CEQ chairs and key agency staff. The bipartisan panel urged President-Elect Obama to reinvigorate the CEQ to help address what they called the current "great environmental crisis."[25] The nation needs a strong CEQ to play the statutory role created for it in NEPA—to shape environmental legislation, to coordinate environmental responses across government, and to give the environment a presence in policy and administration equivalent to that of the economy, as represented by the Council of Economic Advisors.

Similarly, in Chapter 5, we discussed the call to the nation's political leadership in 1996 from two-time EPA Administrator William Ruck-elshaus. He argued forcefully that Congress should avoid the frequent rhetorical attacks and occasional sharp drops in funding that tend to induce "battered agency syndrome."[26] To carry out the nation's environmental policy as set out in statute, the EPA needs enlightened support from political leaders to counteract the agency's natural adversaries in the regulated sectors.

The arguments in favor of robust environmental protection have strong analytic underpinnings. Without intervention, markets cannot independently correct for adverse side effects of economic activity, such as harmful health impacts from air pollution or overexploitation of forests and fisheries in "tragedy of the commons" scenarios. In these situations, prices do not reflect the true costs of the activities, keeping them hidden from participants in the market. This creates perverse incentives for patterns of production and consumption that generate unaccounted-for social and environmental harms and undermine overall well-being. When costs are hidden, cost-benefit analyses, whether in the public or private sector, will err as guideposts for action.

Effective environmental laws and regulations counteract these perverse incentives by increasing the costs of the activities that cause harm. This in turn drives technological innovation and behavioral changes to reduce the previously hidden costs that regulation has made explicit.

Poorly designed policy interventions can do more harm than good. Yet as we described in the previous section of this chapter, policymakers and regulators are learning from experience to develop approaches that can achieve the desired social and environmental goals while limiting economic impact. When well designed and implemented, regulations are a bargain, with benefits outweighing costs. Addressing more complex and larger-scale dilemmas such as climate change and biodiversity loss will require substantially greater capacities in public agencies and private actors. In this context, appropriate funding for the CEQ and the EPA is a good national investment.

The nation has a longstanding commitment to environmental protection. Despite controversy over the costs of regulations, this commitment is unlikely to unravel. Public opinion polling data indicate that for forty years a majority of Americans has consistently listed the environment as an important priority that merits government action and support. The EPA's budget fell sharply during the first years of the Reagan administration and during the Gingrich revolution of the mid-1990s. In both cases, public concerns over antiregulatory overreach ultimately helped the agency's fortunes recover.

In 1996, Republicans in Congress convened hearings to consider eliminating the Department of Energy. Secretary of Energy Hazel O'Leary testified that "the overwhelming majority of programs of the Department of Energy would continue even under the rubric of abolition . . . most of the Department's missions are not discretionary efforts; they are enduring government responsibilities and requirements."[27]

The work of the CEQ and EPA equally falls into the category of "enduring government responsibilities and requirements." The National Environmental Policy Act of 1969 affirms the nation's duty to "fulfill the responsibilities of each generation as trustee of the environment for succeeding generations."[28] We expect that over the next twenty years the CEQ and the EPA—in fits and starts, with rising and falling levels of political and budgetary support, and ultimately with more efficient and equitable environmental policies—will contribute to fulfilling these important responsibilities.

Postscript: Sustainability and the Environmental Protection Agency

In Chapter 7, we completed our formal examination of environmental politics, policy, and administration. In our analysis throughout the book we examined the histories of the Council on Environmental Quality (CEQ) and the Environmental Protection Agency (EPA) as seen through the lens of conceptual agency life cycle models. In this postscript, we step outside this theoretical framework to offer some thoughts on the path U.S. environmental policy and administration have been taking, in halting steps, toward the ambitious processes and goals of sustainability. In considering the practical implications of this emerging realignment of focus, we use climate change as an example.

SUSTAINABILITY

As we discussed in Chapter 2, the National Environmental Policy Act of 1969 (NEPA) was a prescient document helping chart new directions in environmental management both in the United States and globally. Although NEPA does not specifically mention sustainability, the act includes text that clearly anticipates current understanding of the concept, declaring it a policy of the federal government "to create and maintain conditions under which man and nature can exist in productive harmony, and fulfill the social, economic, and other requirements of present and future generations of Americans."[1]

In 1987 the United Nations World Commission on Environment and Development built on this language to define sustainable development as "development that meets the needs of the present without compromising the ability of future generations to meet their own needs."[2] At the 1992 Earth Summit, 178 nations committed to adopting this framework in promoting future development. While this declaration, known as Agenda 21, did not immediately transform global priorities, it did put sustainability on the international agenda. Since then, the Organisation for Economic Co-operation and Development (OECD), a multilateral group of thirty-four nations made up primarily of developed economies, has been particularly active in encouraging member countries to incorporate sustainability into policymaking.

Over the past decade or so, sustainability has become a more visible part of the vocabulary of U.S. environmental policy and administration. In 2004, for example, the EPA announced a new focus on sustainability that included funding to support "regional-scale sustainability projects that are systems-oriented, forward-looking, and preventative."[3] President George W. Bush in 2007 and President Barack Obama in 2009 and 2015 issued executive orders advancing the new agenda. President Obama's 2009 executive order explicitly adopts the original language of NEPA quoted above as the formal definition of sustainability. The 2015 executive order reestablishes the position and office of chief sustainability officer, housing it within the CEQ with funding from the EPA.

In 2011 the National Research Council (NRC) published a report in response to a request from the EPA for guidance in strengthening the analytic and scientific basis for sustainability and integrating sustainability more effectively into the agency's decision making and regulatory actions.[4] The NRC committee focused in part on how to adapt the agency's longstanding analytic emphasis on risk assessment and risk management to be relevant in a new era having sustainability as the overarching goal.

The committee urged the EPA to develop and adopt tools specifically designed to assess implications for sustainability following the example and experience of the OECD. These tools may include, for example, full life cycle analyses of the environmental impacts of products and production processes, cost-benefit analyses that explicitly incorporate environmental aspects typically overlooked in conventional studies, and formal assessments of equity and social justice considerations. Overall, the report recommended a broad, multidisciplinary, participatory approach to regulation that accounts for the "three sustainability pillars," or "triple bottom line," of society, economy, and environment. The EPA accepted the recommendations. Its website now displays a figure (Fig. 8.1) illustrating how the agency works to integrate issues of concern in the three domains.

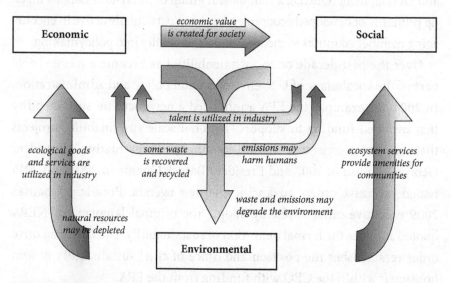

Figure 8.1 Triple Value Model for Sustainable Systems.
NOTE: The EPA explains the graphic as follows: "The sustainability of both the economic system and the social system depend on the availability of services from the environmental system. The services provided by the environmental system, otherwise known as ecosystem services, include provision of food, fuel, materials, water, and energy, as well as flood protection, climate regulation, pollination, and a host of other essential services."
SOURCE: EPA, http://www.epa.gov/sustainability/analytics/.

Among other aspects of interest, Figure 8.1 suggests the key role of industry. Sustainability cannot be achieved solely through government actions. Public policymakers are coming to recognize the importance of public–private partnerships as an essential tool for achieving social and environmental goals, and leaders of many well-managed firms are finding bottom-line and strategic benefits in the adoption of socially and environmentally responsible practices. In growing areas of research, scholars are studying these public and private sector actions and their impacts.[5]

CLIMATE CHANGE

Climate change is a concrete example of a challenging problem of local, national, and global concern that is best understood within the framework of sustainability. Human activities that contribute to climate change, and government and private sector actions aimed at mitigating and adapting to climate change, profoundly affect all three pillars of sustainability: society, economy, and environment. The climate change now occurring can be seen as an indicator or symptom of the current unsustainability of the global economy.[6]

The combustion of fossil fuels is a primary contributor to human-caused climate change. These fuels—coal, petroleum, and natural gas—currently provide approximately 82 percent of the global energy supply.[7] When burned to produce energy they release carbon into the atmosphere in the form of carbon dioxide, a greenhouse gas. Carbon dioxide captures heat energy radiating from the Earth's surface that would otherwise pass out through the atmosphere into space. Additional carbon dioxide added to the atmosphere thus changes the overall energy balance of the Earth system, causing it to warm.

As a direct consequence of fossil fuel combustion over the past two hundred years, the concentration of carbon dioxide in the atmosphere, currently about 400 parts per million by volume, is about 45 percent higher than it was in the preindustrial era. Global carbon dioxide emissions from fossil fuel use currently total about 32 billion tons per year, and the atmospheric concentration of carbon dioxide is rising at a rate of about 2 parts per million per year.[8] Global average surface temperatures over the past century have risen approximately 1.5 degrees Fahrenheit, and worldwide the most recent decade was the warmest on record.[9]

Significant disruptive effects are already occurring.[10] Coastal areas are threatened by rising sea levels. Water supplies, agricultural productivity, and the safety of persons and property are threatened by more energetic storms and changing precipitation patterns. Biodiversity is threatened as marine and terrestrial habitats change more quickly than many species can adapt.

The climate-change issue has several interconnected aspects that make it a challenging policy dilemma. Our economy and material well-being depend on access to affordable and reliable energy supplies, yet the changing climate indicates that our reliance on fossil fuels is unsustainable. We can envision a carbon-neutral energy future, yet it will likely take decades for the necessary transformations in policy, behavior, and technology to take place. There is strong political, economic, and infrastructural inertia built into the current energy-supply system that will slow the necessary changes at the national level, and we lack robust international institutions to coordinate and implement a global response.

SUSTAINABILITY, CLIMATE CHANGE, AND THE EPA

In 2013, the United States emitted approximately 6.7 billion tons of greenhouse gases, just over 20 percent of the global total. As shown in Figure 8.2, 31 percent of U.S. emissions come from electricity generation, 27 percent from transportation, 21 percent from industry, 12 percent from commercial and residential uses, and 9 percent from agriculture. Adjusted for heat-trapping potential, about 82 percent of U.S. greenhouse-gas emissions are in the form of carbon dioxide, primarily from fossil fuel combustion.

Thus fossil fuel combustion is not the only source of U.S. greenhouse-gas emissions, and carbon dioxide is not the only greenhouse gas.

Overview of Greenhouse Gases   Sources of Greenhouse Gas Emissions

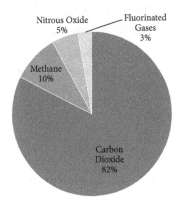
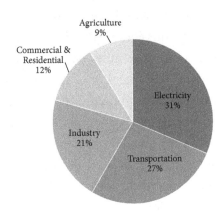

Figure 8.2 U.S. Greenhouse-Gas Emissions by Sector, 2013.
SOURCE: EPA, http://www.epa.gov/climatechange/ghgemissions/usinventory
report.html.

Nonetheless, carbon dioxide from fossil fuels is the primary U.S. contributor to global climate change, so we focus our attention on it here in
reviewing EPA policies in this arena.

Because of variations in their chemical makeup, coal, gasoline, and
natural gas release differing amounts of carbon dioxide per unit of energy
produced.[11] Of the three fuels, natural gas generates the lowest level of
carbon emissions per unit of energy, at about 117 pounds of carbon dioxide per million Btu. Burning gasoline leads to emissions per unit of
energy that are about 35 percent higher than they are for natural gas.
Coal is the most carbon-intensive fuel, with emissions per unit of energy
on average about 90 percent higher than for natural gas. In addition, coal
contains more hazardous impurities, such as sulfur and mercury, which
are also released in combustion. These characteristics of coal—that it is a
high emitter of conventional pollution and of greenhouse gas-pollution—
make it a key focus of both air quality and climate-change regulations.

The EPA under the Obama administration has implemented or is pre-
paring to implement various policies addressing emissions from the four
main sectors: electricity generation, transportation, industry, and com-
mercial/residential uses. For transportation, a key tool is the corporate

average fuel efficiency (CAFE) standard for passenger cars and light-duty trucks. These vehicles account for about 60 percent of transportation-sector emissions.[12] The CAFE policy requires manufacturers to meet overall average-miles-per-gallon benchmarks for the vehicles they sell. The latest tightening of requirements, issued in 2012, sets the average fuel-economy standard at the equivalent of about 54.5 mpg by 2025. Achieving this standard will reduce carbon-dioxide emissions per mile driven by about 35 percent, from about 250 grams per mile in 2016 to about 163 grams per mile in 2025. In addition, the policy will reduce fuel costs for vehicle owners and reduce smog and other forms of unhealthy air pollution.

For energy consumers in industry and the commercial/residential sectors, the EPA works to reduce greenhouse-gas emissions through a range of approaches, many of them involving voluntary, incentive-based programs.[13] Examples include EnergyStar, which certifies energy efficiency for appliances; the Green Power Partnership, which encourages use of non-carbon energy sources such as solar or wind; the Greenhouse Gas Reporting Program, which collects and disseminates emissions data from individual sources; and tax breaks for homeowners if they install such improvements as insulation or energy-efficient windows. The EPA uses similar strategies in the public sector, reducing its own greenhouse-gas emissions and encouraging other government agencies at the federal, state, and local level to do the same. The EPA estimates that these programs in combination reduce emissions by several hundred million tons of carbon dioxide per year.[14]

For the electricity-generation sector, the EPA in 2014 announced a major new administrative rule containing a program for limiting carbon emissions from existing sources.[15] This rule, in the public-comment phase as we write this chapter, includes emission targets for power plants by state. The targets would represent allowable rates of carbon dioxide emissions from fossil fuel fired power plants, accounting for the varying characteristics of states' electricity generation sectors. States could meet the target rates by employing combinations of four main approaches: improving efficiency at existing fossil fuel power plants; relying more heavily on power plants using lower-emitting fossil fuels; expanding use of power plants based on non-carbon fuels, such as nuclear or renewables; and reducing demand by helping consumers improve energy efficiency.[16] States may comply independently or join multistate initiatives, such as regional cap-and-trade programs for carbon emissions. In principle, these flexible rules will allow states to take advantage of opportunities to achieve goals in a cost-effective manner.

In assessing the costs and benefits of the proposed plan, the EPA considers impacts on society, economy, and environment—the three pillars of sustainability. For example, the agency notes that older people, children, and those in poverty will be most affected by changes to climate because they have fewer resources and capacities for adaptation. The agency also accounts for immediate benefits to human health that accompany efforts to mitigate climate change, given that lower greenhouse-gas emissions correlate closely with lower emissions of conventional hazardous air pollutants. Slowing climate change is also expected to help protect biodiversity by reducing threats of extinction. These factors and many others are incorporated into sustainability analyses. Independent scientists are working to confirm the linkages.[17]

Overall the EPA estimates costs of compliance for the proposed program by 2030 to be on the order of about $9 billion per year. Once these costs are accounted for, the agency estimates overall net benefits by 2030—social, economic, and environmental—to be on the order of $50 billion to $80 billion per year.[18]

Despite the large estimated net social benefits, the plan is highly controversial. Those who may be adversely affected are fighting back. Rhetoric is already heated, and the political struggle is likely to get more contentious once the EPA moves to begin implementation. Since coal as a fuel emits the most carbon dioxide per unit of energy produced, the proposed rules in practice will push states to reduce reliance on coal-fired power plants for electricity generation. The coal industry and states where coal is a dominant player in the local economy are working hard to block the proposal. Political polarization between Democrats and Republicans over the issue of climate change in general adds to the tension. Senate Majority

Leader Mitch McConnell of Kentucky, a Republican from a coal state, has promised to use his considerable powers to stop the EPA from implementing the new rules.

Senator McConnell and other opponents of the proposed plan accuse the EPA and the Obama administration of pursuing a "war on coal."[19] They claim that the regulations will cost jobs and raise energy prices. There is some validity in these arguments. Coal is the primary target of the new regulations because coal is the dirtiest fuel that produces the most harmful side effects. The proposed targets will in effect make it more costly to burn coal, because coal combustion will take up a disproportionate share of the emissions allotment. There will be dislocations in the coal sector as states move toward cleaner sources of energy. Electricity costs will rise in the short to medium term as power companies develop new technologies, shift fuels, and restructure in other ways to meet the new targets.

Those opposed to the proposal, however, generally overlook the other side of the equation—that in the aggregate, as indicated by strong estimated net benefits, the society, economy, and environment will be better off with the plan in place. As regulations make it more expensive to burn coal, power generators and consumers will face more directly the social and environmental costs associated with this source of energy that are not otherwise included in its market price. This will create strong incentives to switch to cleaner power.

CONCLUSION

From a sustainability perspective, the United States and the world must move away from carbon-based energy over the next few decades. As this shift occurs, there are certain to be drawn-out struggles over the politics and economics of the transition. In the United States the EPA will be on the front lines and frequently under attack. The agency's mandate to protect human health and the environment requires it to act to reduce emissions from power plants and other sources of pollution that adversely affect air quality and climate stability. Despite net positive outcomes, these actions will attract the ire of those who benefit from the status quo. There are also likely to be ideological battles over the concept of sustainability itself as the approach becomes incorporated more explicitly into U.S. environmental policy and administration. Efforts to balance short-term economic interests with longer-term environmental and social justice objectives will be contested.

Public Law 91–190 91st Congress, S.1075
January 1, 1970

AN ACT

83 STAT. 852

To establish a national policy for the environment, to provide for the establishment of a Council on Environmental Quality, and for other purposes.

Be it enacted by the Senate and House of Representatives of the United States of America in Congress assembled, That this Act may be cited as the "National Environmental Policy Act of 1969."

NATIONAL ENVIRONMENTAL POLICY ACT OF 1969.

PURPOSE

SEC. 2. The purposes of the Act are: To declare a national policy which will encourage productive and enjoyable harmony between man and his environment; to promote efforts which will prevent or eliminate damage to the environment and biosphere and stimulate the health and welfare of man; to enrich the understanding of the ecological systems and natural resources important to the Nation; and to establish a Council on Environmental Quality.

TITLE I

Declaration of National Environmental Policy

POLICIES AND GOALS

Sec. 101. (a) The Congress, recognizing the profound impact of man's activity on the interrelations of all components of the natural environment, particularly the profound influences of population growth, high-density urbanization, industrial expansion, resource exploitation, and new and expanding technological advances and recognizing further the critical importance of restoring and maintaining environmental quality to the overall welfare and development of man, declares that it is the continuing policy of the Federal Government, in cooperation with State and local governments, and other concerned public and private organizations, to use all practicable means and measures, including financial and technical assistance, in a manner calculated to foster and promote the general welfare, to create and maintain conditions under which man and nature can exist in productive harmony, and fulfill the social, economic, and other requirements of present and future generations of Americans.

(b) In order to carry out the policy set forth in this Act, it is the continuing responsibility of the Federal Government to use all practicable means, consistent with other essential considerations of national policy, to improve and coordinate Federal plans, functions, programs, and resources to the end that the Nation may—

(1) fulfill the responsibilities of each generation as trustee of the environment for succeeding generations;

(2) assure for all Americans safe, healthful, productive, and esthetically and culturally pleasing surroundings;

(3) attain the widest range of beneficial uses of the environment without degradation, risk to health or safety, or other undesirable and unintended consequences;

(4) preserve important historic, cultural, and natural aspects of our national heritage, and maintain, wherever possible, an environment which supports diversity and variety of individual choice;

(5) achieve a balance between population and resource use which will permit high standards of living and a wide sharing of life's amenities; and

(6) enhance the quality of renewable resources and approach the maximum attainable recycling of depletable resources.

(c) The Congress recognizes that each person should enjoy a healthful environment and that each person has a responsibility to contribute to the preservation and enhancement of the environment.

ADMINISTRATION

SEC. 102. The Congress authorizes and directs that, to the fullest extent possible: (1) the policies, regulations, and public laws of the United States shall be interpreted and administered in accordance with the policies set forth in this Act, and (2) all agencies of the Federal Government shall—

(A) utilize a systematic, interdisciplinary approach which will insure the integrated use of the natural and social sciences and the environmental design arts in planning and in decision making which may have an impact on man's environment;

(B) identify and develop methods and procedures, in consultation with the Council on Environmental Quality established by title II of this Act, which will insure that presently unquantified environmental amenities and values may be given appropriate consideration in decision-making along with economic and technical considerations;

(C) include in every recommendation or report on proposals
for legislation and other major Federal actions significantly
affecting the quality of the human environment, a detailed
statement by the responsible official on—

    (i) the environmental impact of the proposed action,
    (ii) any adverse environmental effects which cannot be avoided
        should the proposal be implemented,
    (iii) alternatives to the proposed action,
    (iv) the relationship between local short-term uses of man's
        environment and the maintenance and enhancement of
        long-term productivity, and
    (v) any irreversible and irretrievable commitments of resources
        which would be involved in the proposed action should it
        be implemented.

Prior to making any detailed statement, the responsible Federal official
shall consult with and obtain the comments of any Federal agency which
has jurisdiction by law or special expertise with respect to any environmental impact involved. Copies of such statement and the comments and
views of the appropriate Federal, State, and local agencies, which are authorized to develop and enforce environmental standards, shall be made
available to the President, the Council on Environmental Quality and
to the public as provided by section 552 of title 5, United States Code,
and shall accompany the proposal through the existing agency review
processes;
    Copies of statements, etc.; availability.
    81 Stat. 54.

(D) study, develop, and describe appropriate alternatives to
recommended courses of action in any proposal which involves
unresolved conflicts concerning alternative uses of available
resources;

(E) recognize the worldwide and long-range character of
environmental problems and, where consistent with
the foreign policy of the United States, lend appropriate
support to initiatives, resolutions, and programs designed
to maximize international cooperation in anticipating and
preventing a decline in the quality of mankind's world
environment;

(F) make available to States, counties, municipalities,
institutions, and individuals, advice and information useful
in restoring, maintaining, and enhancing the quality of the
environment;

(G) initiate and utilize ecological information in the planning and
development of resource-oriented projects; and

(H) assist the Council on Environmental Quality established by title
II of this Act.

Review.

SEC. 103. All agencies of the Federal Government shall review their
present statutory authority, administrative regulations, and current policies and procedures for the purpose of determining whether there are
any deficiencies or inconsistencies therein which prohibit full compliance
with the purposes and provisions of this Act and shall propose to the
President not later than July 1, 1971, such measures as may be necessary
to bring their authority and policies into conformity with the intent, purposes, and procedures set forth in this Act.

SEC. 104. Nothing in Section 102 or 103 shall in any way affect the
specific statutory obligations of any Federal agency (1) to comply with cri-
teria or standards of environmental quality, (2) to coordinate or consult
with any other Federal or State agency, or (3) to act, or refrain from acting
contingent upon the recommendations or certification of any other Federal or State agency.

SEC. 105. The policies and goals set forth in this Act are supplementary
to those set forth in existing authorizations of Federal agencies.

TITLE II

Council on Environmental Quality

REPORT TO CONGRESS

SEC. 201. The President shall transmit to the Congress annually beginning July 1, 1970, an Environmental Quality Report (hereinafter referred
to as the "report") which shall set forth (1) the status and condition of the
major natural, manmade, or altered environmental classes of the Nation,
including, but not limited to, the air, the aquatic, including marine, estua-
rine, and fresh water, and the terrestrial environment, including, but not
limited to, the forest, dryland, wetland, range, urban, suburban, and rural
environment; (2) current and foreseeable trends in the quality, management and utilization of such environments and the effects of those trends
on the social, economic, and other requirements of the Nation; (3) the ad-
equacy of available natural resources for fulfilling human and economic
requirements of the Nation in the light of expected population pressures;
(4) a review of the programs and activities (including regulatory activities) of the Federal Government, the State and local governments, and
nongovernmental entities or individuals, with particular reference to
their effect on the environment and on the conservation, development
and utilization of natural resources; and (5) a program for remedying the
deficiencies of existing programs and activities, together with recommendations for legislation.

SEC. 202. There is created in the Executive Office of the President a
Council on Environmental Quality (hereinafter referred to as the "Council"). The Council shall be composed of three members who shall be appointed by the President to serve at his pleasure, by and with the advice and
consent of the Senate. The President shall designate one of the members of
the Council to serve as Chairman. Each member shall be a person who, as
a result of his training, experience, and attainments, is exceptionally well
qualified to analyze and interpret environmental trends and information of
all kinds; to appraise programs and activities of the Federal Government in
the light of the policy set forth in title I of this Act; to be conscious of and

responsive to the scientific, economic, social, esthetic, and cultural needs and interests of the Nation; and to formulate and recommend national policies to promote the improvement of the quality of the environment.

COUNCIL ON ENVIRONMENTAL QUALITY

SEC. 203. The Council may employ such officers and employees as may be necessary to carry out its functions under this Act. In addition, the Council may employ and fix the compensation of such experts and consultants as may be necessary for the carrying out of its functions under this Act, in accordance with section 3109 of title 5, United States Code (but without regard to the last sentence thereof).

80 Stat. 416. Duties and functions.

SEC. 204. It shall be the duty and function of the Council—

(1) to assist and advise the President in the preparation of the Environmental Quality Report required by section 201;

(2) to gather timely and authoritative information concerning the conditions and trends in the quality of the environment both current and prospective, to analyze and interpret such information for the purpose of determining whether such conditions and trends are interfering, or are likely to interfere, with the achievement of the policy set forth in title I of this Act, and to compile and submit to the President studies relating to such conditions and trends;

Tasks

(3) to review and appraise the various programs and activities of the Federal Government in the light of the policy set forth in title I of this Act for the purpose of determining the extent to which such programs and activities are contributing to the achievement of such policy, and to make recommendations to the President with respect thereto;

(4) to develop and recommend to the President national policies to foster and promote the improvement of environmental quality to meet the conservation, social, economic, health, and other requirements and goals of the Nation;

(5) to conduct investigations, studies, surveys, research, and analyses relating to ecological systems and environmental quality;

(6) to document and define changes in the natural environment, including the plant and animal systems, and to accumulate necessary data and other information for a continuing analysis of these changes or trends and an interpretation of their underlying causes;

(7) to report at least once each year to the President on the state and condition of the environment; and

(8) to make and furnish such studies, reports thereon, and recommendations with respect to matters of policy and legislation as the President may request.

SEC. 205. In exercising its powers, functions, and duties under this Act, the Council shall—

(1) consult with the Citizens' Advisory Committee on Environmental Quality established by Executive order numbered 11472, dated May 29, 1969, and with such representatives of science, industry, agriculture, labor, conservation organizations, State and local governments and other groups, as it deems advisable; and 34 F. R. 8693.

(2) utilize, to the fullest extent possible, the services, facilities, and information (including statistical information) of public and private agencies and organizations, and individuals, in order that duplication of effort and expense may be avoided, thus assuring that the Council's activities will not unnecessarily overlap or conflict with similar activities authorized by law and performed by established agencies.

SEC. 206. Members of the Council shall serve full time and the Chairman of the Council shall be compensated at the rate provided for Level II of the Executive Schedule Pay Rates (5 U.S.C. 5313). The other members of the Council shall be compensated at the rate provided for Level IV or the Executive Schedule Pay Rates (5 U.S.C. 5315).

Tenure and compensation. 80 Stat. 460, 461.

Sᴇᴄ. 207. There are authorized to be appropriated to carry out the provisions of this Act not to exceed $300,000 for fiscal year 1970, $700,000 for fiscal year 1971, and $1,000,000 for each fiscal year thereafter.

81 Stat. 638.

Appropriations.

Approved January 1, 1970.

LEGISLATIVE HISTORY

ʜᴏᴜsᴇ ʀᴇᴘᴏʀᴛs	No. 91–378, 91–378, pt. 2, accompanying H. R. 12549 (Comm. on Merchant Marine & Fisheries) and 91–765 (Comm. of Conference).
sᴇɴᴀᴛᴇ ʀᴇᴘᴏʀᴛ	No. 91–296 (Comm. on Interior & Insular Affairs).

ᴄᴏɴɢʀᴇssɪᴏɴᴀʟ ʀᴇᴄᴏʀᴅ, Vol. 115 (1969):

July 10:	Considered and passed Senate.
Sept. 23:	Considered and passed House, amended, in lieu of H. R. 12549.
Oct. 8:	Senate disagreed to House amendments; agreed to conference.
Dec. 20:	Senate agreed to conference report.
Dec. 22:	House agreed to conference report.

Figure 1.1 in Chapter 1 shows the organization table for the U.S. government.[1] The Constitution is listed at the top, and the three branches of government established by the Constitution—legislative, executive, and judicial—are presented in boxes below the Constitution. Located in the box titled "Executive Branch" are the president, the vice president, and the Executive Office of the President (EOP).

The EOP was established in 1939 and currently has thirteen agencies that serve the president. The White House Office and the Office of Budget and Management (OMB; originally named the Bureau of the Budget) were placed in the EOP in 1939.[2] The White House Office is where many of the president's personal staff assistants are located. The OMB prepares the president's annual budget request, which is presented to Congress as *The Budget of the United States*. Other highly visible entities that currently exist within the EOP include the National Security Council, which was placed in the EOP in 1949.

Both the president and Congress can place entities in the EOP. Congress established the Council of Economic Advisers in 1949 and placed it in the EOP. Twenty years later, in 1969, Congress created the Council on Environmental Quality and put it in the EOP. Some of the agencies placed in the EOP between 1939 and 2008 have remained there over time, while others have been abolished, lie dormant, or were transferred to other executive branch organizations.[3]

The Cabinet departments, now fifteen in number, are presented in the two rows located just below the EOP in Figure 1.1. The line connecting those departments to the president indicates a formal, hierarchical or reporting relationship. The fifteen Cabinet departments vary substantially in age, size, and function, but in combination these departments represent almost 90 percent of all U.S. government employees and account for almost 80 percent of total spending.[4]

The number of Cabinet departments, the names of some departments, and the functions or entities that exist within those departments have changed over time. The national government's pollution-abatement and -control programs were located in the Department of Health, Education, and Welfare (HEW) until December of 1970. Then, as part of President Nixon's Reorganization Plan No. 3, those programs were formally transferred to the newly created Environmental Protection Agency (EPA).

In 1980, HEW was affected by another reorganization. In this reorganization, initiated by President Carter and approved by Congress, "education" programs (the "E" in HEW) were removed and placed in a newly created Department of Education. Consequently, HEW was renamed Health and Human Services.

In addition to EOP and the Cabinet departments, there are three other types of executive branch organizations. These entities are listed at the bottom of Figure 1.1 in a box titled "Independent Establishments and Government Corporation." A total of fifty-seven entities are included in this cluster.

These fifty-seven entities can be subdivided into three groups: independent regulatory boards and commissions, government corporations, and other independent agencies. The EPA is part of the third group; it is an independent agency. The common denominator among the organizations labeled "other independent agencies" is that they are not part of the EOP, and they are not Cabinet departments, independent regulatory boards, or government corporations.

PREFACE

1. James K. Conant, "The Changing Face of the New Jersey Department of Environmental Protection." *The Environmental Forum* 4, no.8 (1985), 45–53; and James K. Conant, "Stability, Change and Leadership in State Administration: 1970–1986." *State and Local Government Review* 21, no. 1 (1989), 3–10.
2. Peter J. Balint, Ronald E. Stewart, Anand Desai, and Lawrence C. Walters, *Wicked Environmental Problems: Managing Uncertainty and Conflict* (Washington, D.C.: Island Press, 2011).

CHAPTER 1

1. Our decision to begin work on this book was inspired by the fact that 2010 was the fortieth anniversary of what is now commonly described as the "year of the environment"—1970.
2. A summary of pre-1970 national government legislation can be found in Council on Environmental Quality, *Environmental Quality: The First Annual Report of the Council on Environmental Quality* (Washington, D.C.: U.S. Government Printing Office, 1970), Chapters III, IV, and VI, http://www.slideshare.net/whitehouse/august-1970-environmental-quality-the-first-annual-report-of. One example of the legislation is the Water Pollution Control Act of 1956 and subsequent amendments in 1961, 1965, and 1966.
3. Council on Environmental Quality, *Environmental Quality: The First Annual Report*, 75–76.
4. National Environmental Policy Act of 1969, P.L. 91–190, *U.S. Statutes at Large* 83 (1970) 852. The full text of the law is presented in Appendix 1.
5. If an agency is created in statutory law, both chambers of Congress must pass the same bill. Then, the bill must be signed into law by the president. By using a reorganization plan, President Nixon skipped the standard legislative process by submitting to Congress a plan for creating the EPA by modifying existing organizational arrangements. Because Congress did not formally object to President Nixon's plan within 30 days, the reorganization went into effect.
6. House of Representatives, Document No. 91–366, *Reorganization Plan No. 3 of 1970*, submitted by the President of the United States, July 9, 1970, referred to the Committee on Government Operations. Available at http://www2.epa.gov/aboutepa/reorganization-plan-no-3-1970 (accessed August 15, 2013).

7. The formal title of the Commission was the President's Advisory Council on Executive Organization. President Nixon created the council on April 15, 1969, and appointed Roy Ash as chairman. The formal title of the document the Commission submitted to the President on April 29, 1970, was "Federal Organization for Environmental Protection." Additional documentation is available at http://www.nixonlibrary.gov/forresearchers/find/textual/central/smof/paceo.php.

8. One of the first recommendations the newly established CEQ made to the president was the creation of an environmental-protection agency. See Council on Environmental Quality, *Environmental Quality: The First Annual Report of the Council on Environmental Quality* (Washington, D.C.: U.S. Government Printing Office, 1970).

9. Jack Lewis, "The Birth of the EPA." *EPA Journal* 1 (1985). Available at http://www2.epa.gov/aboutepa/birth-epa (accessed August 25, 2013).

10. *Clean Air Act Amendments of 1970*, Public Law 91–604. *U.S Statutes at Large* 84 (1970): 1676.

11. In conducting the research for this book, we drew on the existing literature on NEPA, the CEQ, and the EPA. Relevant books and articles by insiders with direct knowledge include those by Lynton K. Caldwell, who worked for Senator Henry "Scoop" Jackson during the formulation and passage of NEPA; James G. (Gus) Speth, who was first a member and then chair of the CEQ during the Carter administration; Dinah Bear, who served at the CEQ almost the entire period from 1981 to 2007, first as deputy counsel and then as general counsel; and Ray Clark, who was senior policy analyst and associate director of the CEQ from 1992 to 1999. Other relevant publications by scholars who were not directly involved with the creation or management of NEPA, the CEQ, and the EPA include those by Frederick R. Anderson, Matthew J. Lindstrom and Zachery A. Smith, and Marc K. Landy, Marc J. Roberts, and Stephen R. Thomas. There are also a host of other works that include discussions of NEPA, the CEQ, and the EPA.

12. We have previously published two studies using this approach. The first was James K. Conant and Peter J. Balint, "The Council on Environmental Quality at 40: A Life Cycle Analysis." *Environmental Practice* 13 no. 2 (2011): 113–121. The second publication was Peter J. Balint and James K. Conant, "The Environmental Protection Agency's Budget from 1970–2010: A Life cycle Analysis." *Public Budgeting and Finance* 33 no. 4, (2013): 22–42.

13. These four organization life-cycle models are commonly mentioned in the public administration literature.

14. Caldwell, *The National Environmental Policy Act: An Agenda for the Future.*

15. Council on Environmental Quality, *Environmental Quality: The First Annual Report*, 25.

16. In the EIS process, all of the executive-branch departments and agencies of the national government were required to identify actions, or potential future actions, that might adversely effect the environment.

17. Lynton K. Caldwell, "Implementing NEPA: A Non-Technical Political Task," in *Environmental Policy and NEPA: Past, Present, and Future*, ed. E. Ray Clark and Larry W. Canter (Boca Raton, FL: St. Lucie Press, 1997), 25–50.

18. The Government Accounting Office, Report of the Comptroller General of the United States: *The Council on Environmental Quality: A Tool for Shaping National Policy*, CEC-81-66, March 19, 1981.

19. James Q. Wilson, *Bureaucracy: What Government Agencies Do and Why They Do It* (New York: Basic Books, 1989).

20. The origin of this quote is uncertain. The *Yale Book of Quotations* (New Haven, CT: Yale University Press, 2006), 92, offers the following information: "Attributed [to Neils Bohr] in Mark Kac, 'Statistics' (1975). Kac states that this may have been 'an old Danish proverb.' K. K. Steincke, *Goodbye and Thanks* (1948), quotes it as a pun used in the Danish Parliament in the late 1930s."

CHAPTER 2

1. National Environmental Policy Act of 1969 (P.L. 91–190, *U.S. Statutes at Large* 83 [1970]), 852. The full text of the law is presented in Appendix 1.

2. See Figure 1.1 for the location of the Executive Office of the President within the Executive Branch.

3. National Environmental Policy Act of 1969.

4. United Nations World Commission on Environment and Development, *Our Common Future* (New York: Oxford University Press, 1987).

5. Nicholas A. Robinson, *NEPA at 40: International Dimensions*. Pace Law Faculty Publications, Paper 575 (2009), http://digitalcommons.pace.edu/lawfaculty/575.

6. Council on Environmental Quality, *Environmental Quality: The First Annual Report of the Council on Environmental Quality* (Washington, D.C.: U.S. Government Printing Office, 1970), 5, http://www.slideshare.net/whitehouse/august-1970-environmental-quality-the-first-annual-report-of.

7. National Archives and Records Administration, "Act creating Yellowstone National Park, March 1, 1872"; Enrolled Acts and Resolutions of Congress, 1789–1996; General Records of the United States Government; Record Group 11; National Archives, http://www.ourdocuments.gov/doc.php?doc=45.

8. For a review of the literature on this topic, see Soumyananda Dinda, "Environmental Kuznets Curve Hypothesis: A Survey." *Ecological Economics* 49, no. 4 (2004), 431–455. For a critique, see David I. Stern, "The Rise and Fall of the Environmental Kuznets Curve." *World Development* 32, no. 8 (2004), 1419–1439.

9. Rachel Carson, *Silent Spring* (Boston, MA: Houghton Mifflin, 1962).

10. The Apollo 8 astronauts were Frank Borman, James Lovell, and William Anders. A careful review of the history of this photograph can be found in Fred Spier, "The Elusive Apollo 8 Earthrise Photo," http://www.ibhanet.org/resources/documents/newsletters/spierearthrisephoto.pdf.

11. John Noble Wilford, "On Hand for Space History as Superpowers Spar." *New York Times*, July 14, 2009, http://www.nytimes.com/2009/07/14/science/space/14mission.html?emc=eta1.

12. Archibald MacLeish, "Riders on Earth Together, Brothers in Eternal Cold." *New York Times*, December 25, 1968, http://www.nytimes.com/2008/12/24/opinion/24wed4.html?emc=eta1.

13. Quoted in Keith C. Clarke and Jeffrey J. Hemphill, "The Santa Barbara Oil Spill, A Retrospective," in *Yearbook of the Association of Pacific Coast Geographers, Vol. 64*, ed. Darrick Danta (Honolulu: University of Hawai'i Press, 2002), 157–162, http://www.geog.ucsb.edu/~kclarke/Papers/SBOilSpill1969.pdf.

14. Tom Wicker, *One of Us: Richard Nixon and the American Dream* (New York: Random House, 1991).

15. Frederick R. Anderson, *NEPA in the Courts: A Legal Analysis of the National Environmental Policy Act* (Washington, D.C.: Resources for the Future Press, 1973).

16. Lynton K. Caldwell, *The National Environmental Policy Act: An Agenda for the Future* (Bloomington: Indiana University Press, 1998).

17. Jack Lewis, "The Birth of the EPA." *EPA Journal* (November 1985), http://www2.epa.gov/aboutepa/birth-epa.

18. Wicker, *One of Us*.

19. Council on Environmental Quality, *First Annual Report*, 5. On the opening page of its first annual report, the CEQ said: "Historians may one day call 1970 the year of the year of the environment." They were correct in their prediction—that is how it has worked out.

20. Daniel J. Fiorino, *The New Environmental Regulation* (Boston, MA: MIT Press, 2006).

21. Environmental Protection Agency, *National Summary of State Information*, "Watershed Assessment, Tracking & Environmental Results," http://ofmpub.epa.gov/waters10/attains_nation_cy.control#prob_surv_states.

22. National Research Council, *Achieving Nutrient and Sediment Reduction Goals in the Chesapeake Bay: An Evaluation of Program Strategies and Implementation* (Washington, D.C.: The National Academies Press, 2011), http://www.nap.edu/catalog.php?record_id=13,131.

23. David R. Steward et al., "Tapping Unsustainable Groundwater Stores for Agricultural Production in the High Plains Aquifer of Kansas, Projections to 2110." *Proceedings of the National Academy of Sciences* 110, no. 37 (2013): E3477–E3486.

24. David Malakoff, "The Gas Surge." *Science* 344, no. 6191 (2014), 1464–1467.

25. Michael E. Kraft, *Environmental Policy and Politics*, 5th ed. (Boston, MA: Longman, 2011).

26. It is worth noting, however, that one of the trade-offs associated with capturing air pollutants with scrubbers, electrostatic precipitators, and so forth before they exit large utility stacks is that the captured pollutants have to go somewhere, so they are put into the land and water.

27. For details on health effects and sources of these pollutants, see Environmental Protection Agency, "Six Common Pollutants," http://www.epa.gov/air/urbanair/.

28. For details on emissions and ambient air quality trends, see Environmental Protection Agency, "Air Quality Trends," http://www.epa.gov/airtrends/aqtrends.html#comparison.

29. Environmental Protection Agency, *Fact Sheet: EPA's Revised Particulate Matter Standards*, July 17, 1997, http://www.epa.gov/ttn/oarpg/t1/fact_sheets/pmfact.pdf.

30. Environmental Protection Agency, "Air Quality Trends."

31. Environmental Protection Agency, *The Benefits and Costs of the Clean Air Act, 1970 to 1990*, October 1997, http://www.epa.gov/cleanairactbenefits/copy.html.

32. See, for example, Paul R. Portney, "Air Pollution Policy," in *Public Policies for Environmental Protection*, 2nd ed., ed. Paul R. Portney and Robert N. Stavins (Washington, D.C.: Resources for the Future, 2000), 77–124; A. Myrick Freeman III, "Environmental Policy Since Earth Day I: What Have We Gained?" *Journal of Economic Perspectives* 16, no. 1 (2002), 125–146.

33. Louraine G. Chesnut and David M. Mills, "A Fresh Look at the Benefits and Costs of the US Acid Rain Program." *Journal of Environmental Management* 77, no. 3 (2005), 252–266.

CHAPTER 3

1. For example, Woodrow Wilson, "The Study of Administration." *Political Science Quarterly* 2, no. 2 (1887), 209.

2. This view is now widely held in the public policy, public administration, and policy implementation literature. See for example Denise Scheberle, *Federalism and Environmental Policy: Trust and the Politics of Implementation* (Washington, D.C.: Georgetown University Press, 2004).

3. See for example Barry Bozeman, "The Effect of Economic and Partisan Change on Federal Appropriations." *Western Political Quarterly* 30, no. 1 (1977), 112–124; D. Roderick Kiewiet and Mathew D. McCubbins, "Appropriations Decisions as a Bilateral Bargaining Game between President and Congress." *Legislative Studies Quarterly* 10, no. 2 (1985), 181–201; Christopher Wlezien, "Patterns of Representation: Dynamics of Public Preferences and Policy." *Journal of Politics* 66, no. 1 (2004), 1–24.

4. For example, Gerald Auten, Barry Bozeman, and Robert Cline, "A Sequential Model of Congressional Appropriations." *American Journal of Political Science* 28, no. 3 (1984), 503–523.

5. For example, Otto A. Davis, M. A. H. Dempster, and Aaron Wildavsky, "The Politics of the Budgetary Process." *American Political Science Review* 60, no. 3 (1966), 529–547.

6. Auten, Bozeman, and Cline, "A Sequential Model."

7. M. A. H. Dempster, Aaron Wildavsky, and Otto Davis, "Toward a Predictive Theory of Government Expenditure: US Domestic Appropriations." *British Journal of Political Science* 4, no. 4 (1974): 419–452.

8. Jonathan R. Tompkins, *Organization Theory and Public Management* (Belmont, CA: Thomson Wadsworth, 2005), 240, reports that Ludwig von Bertalanffy "urged the study of living things as organic wholes in 1920, introduced the theory of the organism as an open system in 1940, and established the field of general systems theory in 1945."

9. Anthony Downs, *Inside Bureaucracy* (Boston, MA: Little Brown, 1967).

10. Downs's primary focus, however, seems to be on governmental bureaus or organizations, rather than on private sector or nonprofit organizations.

11. Downs, *Inside Bureaucracy*, 9. Unfortunately, Downs does not provide specific information about what metrics could be used to define what constitutes an "initial survival threshold."

12. *Ibid.*, 10.
13. *Ibid.*
14. Peter F. Drucker, *The Age of Discontinuity: Guidelines to Our Changing Society* (London: Heinemann, 1969).
15. Herbert Kaufman, *The Limits of Organizational Change* (Tuscaloosa: University of Alabama Press, 1972).
16. Herbert Kaufmann, *Are Government Organizations Immortal?* (Washington, D.C.: Brookings, 1976).
17. *Ibid.*, 25.
18. *Ibid.*, 28.
19. *Ibid.*
20. *Ibid.*, 23
21. *Ibid.*, 24
22. David E. Lilienthal, *TVA—Democracy on the March* (New York: Penguin, 1944).
23. Philip Selznick, *TVA and the Grass Roots: A Study in the Sociology of Formal Organization* (Berkeley: University of California Press, 1949).
24. Louis C. Gawthrop, *Public Service and Democracy: Ethical Imperatives for the 21st Century* (New York: Chatham House, 1998). The story of the birth, important work, and death of this organization is contained in the chapter titled "A Vision of the Common Good."
25. As reported by Gawthrop, *Public Service*, 107, the three primary policy goals of the agency were "(1) to restore land ownership through the allocation of low-interest loans to farmers who were burdened with marginal or inadequate land; (2) to restore the productivity of ruined land through soil conversation and rebuilding projects, and (3) to resettle—that is to relocate, rehabilitate, and renew—farm families whose agricultural livelihood had been destroyed by the Depression."
26. *Ibid.*, 119.
27. James Q. Wilson, *Bureaucracy: What Government Agencies Do and Why They Do It* (New York: Basic Books, 1989).
28. James K. Conant, "The Changing Face of the New Jersey Department of Environmental Protection." *The Environmental Forum* 4, no. 8 (1985), 45–53; and James K. Conant, "Stability, Change and Leadership in State Administration: 1970–1986." *State and Local Government Review* 21, no. 1 (1989), 3–10.
29. Daniel P. Carpenter, "Stochastic Prediction and Estimation of Nonlinear Political Durations: An Application to the Lifetime of Bureaus," in *Political Complexity: Nonlinear Models of Politics*, ed. D. Richards (Ann Arbor: University of Michigan Press, 2000), 209–238; David E. Lewis, "The Politics of Agency Termination: Confronting the Myth of Agency Immortality." *Journal of Politics* 64, no. 1 (2002), 89–107; Daniel P. Carpenter and David E. Lewis, "Political Learning from Rare Events: Poisson Inference, Fiscal Constraints and the Lifetime of Bureaus." *Political Analysis* 12, no. 3 (2004): 201–232.
30. Lewis, "Politics of Agency Termination," 90.
31. Ronald Reagan, *Inaugural Address*, January 20, 1981, http://www.presidency.ucsb.edu/ws/?pid=43,130.

32. Norman J. Vig, "Presidential Leadership and the Environment," in *Environmental Policy: New Directions for the Twenty-First Century*, 6th ed., ed. Norman J. Vig and Michael E. Kraft (Washington, D.C.: CQ Press, 2006), pp. 100–123; Michael E. Kraft, "Environmental Policy in Congress," in *Environmental Policy: New Directions for the Twenty-First Century*, 6th ed., ed. Norman J. Vig and Michael E. Kraft (Washington, D.C.: CQ Press, 2006), pp. 124–147.

33. Charles E. Lindblom, "The Science of 'Muddling Through.'" *Public Administration Review* 19, no. 2 (1959), 79–88.

34. David Braybrooke and Charles E. Lindblom, *A Strategy of Decision: Policy Evaluation as Social Process* (New York: Free Press, 1963).

35. Charles E. Lindblom, *The Intelligence of Democracy: Decision Making through Mutual Adjustments* (New York: Free Press, 1965).

36. Davis, Dempster, and Wildavsky, " The Politics of the Budgetary Process."

37. Dempster, Wildavsky, and Davis, " Toward a Predictive Theory of Government Expenditure: US Domestic Appropriations."

38. Auten, Bozeman, and Cline, " A Sequential Model."

39. *Ibid.*, 505.

40. *Ibid.*, 503.

41. *Ibid.*, 505.

42. *Ibid.*, 503.

43. Anthony Downs, "Up and Down with Ecology—The 'Issue-Attention Cycle.'" *Public Interest* 28 (1972), 38–50.

44. *Ibid.*, 38.

45. *Ibid.*

46. Ibid., 39.

47. *Ibid.*

48. *Ibid.*, 41.

49. *Ibid.*, 45. All quotations in this paragraph are taken from this page.

50. Andrew Kohut, "But What Do the Polls Show," in *The Politics of News: The News of Politics*, ed. Doris A. Graber, Dennis McQuail, and Pippa Norris (Washington, D.C.: CQ Press, 2007).

51. *Ibid.*, 2.

52. *Ibid.*, 7.

CHAPTER 4

1. *National Environmental Policy Act of 1969* (P.L. 91–190), *U.S. Statutes at Large* 83 (1970): 52. The full text of the National Environmental Policy Act is provided in Appendix 1.

2. *Environmental Quality: The First Annual Report of the Council on Environmental Quality*, (Washington, D.C.: U.S. Government Printing Office, 1970), 325–326.

3. *Ibid.*, 93–104.

4. U.S. General Accounting Office, *The Council on Environmental Quality: A Tool in Shaping National Policy*, Report by the Comptroller General of the United States, CED-81-66 (Washington, D.C.: U.S. General Accounting Office, 1980), 6; 20 pp. Available at http://archive.gao.gov/f0102/114638.pdf (accessed April 28, 2011).

5. This view is corroborated in the following quotation, which appears on the cover page of the 1981 General Accounting Office report cited above: "the Council on Environmental Quality is a relatively small body in the Executive Office of the President . . . CEQ, nevertheless has much influence over national environmental policy. CEQ serves as an environmental advisor to the President and to the Congress—a unique role that many believe could not be fulfilled effectively by another agency."

6. *Environmental Quality: The First Annual Report of the Council on Environmental Quality*, 25–28.

7. Lee Talbot, 2009. Personal communication. Professor, Department of Environmental Science and Policy, George Mason University, Fairfax, VA; former chief science advisor to the CEQ, January 8.

8. *Ibid.*

9. A list of the staff members and biographical information about each can be found in *Environmental Quality: The First Annual* Report: 324–327.

10. Lee Talbot, 2009.

11. Norman J. Vig, "Presidential Leadership and the Environment," in *Environmental Policy: New Directions for the Twenty-First Century*, 6th ed., ed. Norman J. Vig and Michael E. Kraft (Washington D.C.: CQ Press, 2006), 100–123.

12. Council on Environmental Quality (CEQ), *The Global 2000 Report to the President: Entering the Twenty-First Century* (Washington, D.C.: U.S. Government Printing Office, 1980), 416.

13. One potential explanation for this circumstance is that the president and White House staff preferred to work with one person at the CEQ (the chair), rather than a chair and two other members. Another potential explanation is that it was difficult for the Reagan White House staff, who did not want the CEQ to actively pursue solutions to environmental problems, to find potential nominees with an anti-environmental ideology who met the qualifications required in NEPA. Caldwell (1998) reports that the official rationale the Reagan administration offered for this change was the Sunshine Act of 1976. This Act required open meetings of government panels, which might have complicated CEQ's proceedings if the CEQ had more than one member.

14. George H.W. Bush, *Acceptance Speech, 1988 Republican National Convention*. George Bush Presidential Library and Museum, College Station, TX. Available at http://bushlibrary.tamu.edu/research/pdfs/rnc.pdf (accessed April 28, 2011).

15. Public Broadcasting Service (PBS), *American Experience: George H.W. Bush*. PBS, Arlington, VA, 2011. Available at http://www.pbs.org/wgbh/amex/bush41/more/domestic.html (accessed April 28, 2011).

16. David Remnick, "Ozone Man." *New Yorker*, April 24, 2008. Available at http://www.newyorker.com/archive/2006/04/24/060424ta_talk_remnick (accessed April 28, 2011).

17. Ronald C. Moe, "The 'Reinventing Government' Exercise: Misinterpreting the Problem, Misjudging the Consequences." *Public Administration Review* 54, no. 2 (2006), 111–122.

18. Linton K. Caldwell, *The National Environmental Policy Act: An Agenda for the Future* (Bloomington: Indiana University Press, 1998), 232.

19. Dinah Bear, "The National Environmental Policy Act: Its Origins and Evolutions." *Natural Resources and Environment* 10, no. 2 (1995), 3–6, 69–73.

20. *The Paperwork Reduction Act of 1995* (Public Law 104–13), *U.S. Statutes at Large* 109 (1995): 163.

21. Milo Mason, "Interview: James L. Connaughton," *Natural Resources and Environment* 23, no. 2 (2008), 36–39.

22. Andrew C. Revkin, and Matthew L. Wald, "Former Bush White House Aide Defends Edits to Global Warming Reports." *New York Times*, March 20, 2007. Available at http://www.nytimes.com/2007/03/20/world/americas/20iht-climate.4966561.html (accessed April 23, 2011).

23. *Ibid.*

24. Dinah Bear, Ray Clark, William M. Cohen, Mark S. Davis, Michael R. Deland, Robert Dreher, George Frampton, Oliver A. Houck, Thomas C. Jensen, Nathaniel S.W. Lawrence, Kathleen McGinty, Roger Schlickeisen, James Gustav Speth, David Struhs, James Strock, Russel E. Train, James T.B. Tripp, Brook B. Yeager, and Nicholas C. Yost, *Facing the Future: Recommendations on the White House Council on Environmental Quality—A Report to the President-Elect* (New Orleans, LA: Tulane Institute on Water Resources Law and Policy, Tulane Law School, 2008), 18 pp. Available at http://www.law.tulane.edu/uploadedFiles/Institutes_and_Centers/Water_Resources_Law_and_Policy/Documents/Facing%20the%20Future.pdf (accessed September 2, 2010).

25. In contemporary circumstances, a private sector consulting firm that can perform the "social mission" may be a competitor, and it may be the preferred choice of a president or congressional appropriators.

CHAPTER 5

1. Jack Lewis, "The Birth of the EPA," *EPA Journal* (November 1985), http://www2.epa.gov/aboutepa/birth-epa.

2. For example, Herbert Kaufman, *Are Government Organizations Immortal?* (Washington, D.C.: Brookings, 1976); Daniel P. Carpenter and David E. Lewis, "Political Learning from Rare Events: Poisson Inference, Fiscal Constraints, and the Lifetime of Bureaus," *Political Analysis* 12, no. 3 (2004), 201–332.

3. For example, Norman J. Vig and Michael E. Kraft, "Appendix 2," in *Environmental Policy*, 8th ed., ed. Norman J. Vig and Michael E. Kraft (Thousand Oaks, CA: CQ Press, 2013), 404. The EPA budget data used in our study are from the annual presidents' budgets: Office of Management and Budget, *Budget of the United States Government*, Federal Reserve Archives, http://fraser.stlouisfed.org/publication/?pid=54. Each year, the president's budget contains proposed budgetary authority for all agencies for the upcoming fiscal year, estimates for the current year and previous year, and actual values for two years prior. In compiling our dataset, we used the actual budget for each fiscal year as reported in the president's budget from two years later. To ensure comparable numbers from a consistent source, the most recent year in our dataset is FY 2010, taken from the FY

2012 budget. In adjusting for inflation, we used the CPI inflation calculator of the Bureau of Labor Statistics, http://www.bls.gov/data/inflation_calculator.htm.

4. Richard M. Nixon, "Annual Message to the Congress on the State of the Union," January 22, 1970, http://www.presidency.ucsb.edu/ws/?pid=2921.

5. Richard M. Nixon, " Title 5, Appendix—Reorganization Plan No. 3 of 1970," July 9, 1970 (Washington, D.C.: U.S. Government Printing Office, 1971), 202–207, http://www.gpo.gov/fdsys/pkg/USCODE-2011-title5/pdf/USCODE-2011-title5-app-reorganiz-other-dup92.pdf.

6. Richard M. Nixon, "Special Message to the Congress about Reorganization Plans to Establish the Environmental Protection Agency and the National Oceanic and Atmospheric Administration," July 9, 1970, in *Public Papers of the Presidents of the United States: Richard M. Nixon 1970* (Washington, D.C.: U.S. Government Printing Office, 1971), 582, http://quod.lib.umich.edu/p/ppotpus/4731750.1970.001?view=toc.

7. Nixon, " Special Message," 578.

8. Jon Agnone, "Amplifying Public Opinion: The Policy Impact of the U.S. Environmental Movement." *Social Forces* 85, no. 4 (2007), 1593–1620.

9. Michael E. Kraft and Norman J. Vig, "Environmental Policy over Four Decades," in *Environmental Policy*, 8th ed., ed. Norman J. Vig and Michael E. Kraft (Thousand Oaks, CA: CQ Press, 2013), 2–29.

10. Nixon, " Special Message," 578.

11. *Ibid.*, 581.

12. For instance, Don Young, "Obama's EPA as an Employment Prevention Agency." *Politico*, March 15, 2012, http://www.politico.com/news/stories/0312/74072.html.

13. Dennis C. Williams, "The Guardian: EPA's Formative Years, 1970–1973," EPA Doc. No. 202-K-93-002, September 1993, http://www2.epa.gov/aboutepa/guardian-epas-formative-years-1970-1973.

14. For data sources, see footnote 3 in this chapter. The value for 1970 represents the combined budget for activities in other agencies aggregated under the EPA's jurisdiction in 1971. The value for 1971 reflects the sizable increase that occurred as the EPA became a freestanding entity and took on new responsibilities under the Clean Air Act of 1970.

15. William D. Ruckelshaus, "Stopping the Pendulum." *Environmental Toxicology and Chemistry* 15, no. 3 (1996), 229–232.

16. General Social Survey data from General Social Survey, http://www3.norc.org/GSS+Website/; Gallup data from Gallup, "Environment," http://www.gallup.com/poll/1615/environment.aspx#1; Cambridge data from Riley E. Dunlap and Rik Scarce, "Poll Trends: Environmental Problems and Protection." *Public Opinion Quarterly* 55, no. 4 (1991): 651–672. See footnotes 29 and 30 in this chapter, and the accompanying text in the section titled "Variables that Might Explain the Changes in the EPA's Budget," for details on survey questions, missing data, and the computation of trend-line values.

17. Robin Toner, "Bush, in Enemy Waters, Says Rival Hindered Cleanup of Boston Harbor." *New York Times*, September 2, 1988, http://www.nytimes.com/1988/09/02/us/bush-in-enemy-waters-says-rival-hindered-cleanup-of-boston-harbor.html.

18. Diane J. Heith, *Polling to Govern: Public Opinion and Presidential Leadership* (Stanford, CA: Stanford University Press, 2004), 112.

19. Martin Carcasson, "Prudence, Procrastination, or Politics: George Bush and the Earth Summit of 1992," in *The Rhetorical Presidency of George H. W. Bush*, ed. Marin J. Medhurst (College Station, TX: Texas A&M University Press, 2006), 119–148.

20. For data sources, see footnote 3 in this chapter. The years 1970 and 1971 are omitted in Figure 5.3 because the EPA was established during FY 1971; 1972 is omitted because in measuring the variable as the change from one year to the next there is no value for the first year in the series.

21. Particularly the problem of autocorrelation of error terms in regressions using time-series data.

22. Standard deviation = 9.96.

23. The z scores for the 1975 increase and the 1982 decrease are 2.4 and −2.6, respectively.

24. For example, Barry Bozeman, "The Effect of Economic and Partisan Change on Federal Appropriations." *Western Political Quarterly* 30, no. 1 (1977), 112–124; D. Roderick Kiewiet and Mathew D. McCubbins, "Appropriations Decisions as a Bilateral Bargaining Game between President and Congress." *Legislative Studies Quarterly* 10, no. 2 (1985), 181–201; Christopher Wlezien, "Patterns of Representation: Dynamics of Public Preferences and Policy." *Journal of Politics* 66, no. 1 (2004), 1–24.

25. We drew data on the party makeup of Congress from the websites of the House (http://history.house.gov/Institution/Party-Divisions/Party-Divisions/) and Senate (http://www.senate.gov/pagelayout/history/one_item_and_teasers/partydiv.htm). We drew data on unemployment from the Bureau of Labor Statistics (http://www.bls.gov/data/#unemployment), on gross domestic product from the Bureau of Economic Analysis (http://www.bea.gov/national/index.htm#gdp), and on federal nondefense discretionary spending from the Congressional Budget Office, Historical Budget Data (http://www.cbo.gov/publication/21999). For the political and economic variables, we experimented with lagged and unlagged values, although in general lagging by one year is appropriate as budgets for a given fiscal year are likely to be affected by conditions in the prior year. We included the variable for nondefense discretionary spending in the form of percent change from the previous year unlagged, because the idea is that the EPA's budget may respond to the same broad pressures that drive changes in nondefense discretionary spending generally, both in a given year and over time. See Agnone, "Amplifying Public Opinion"; and Wlezien, "Patterns of Representation."

26. Wlezien, "Patterns of Representation," 2.

27. *Ibid.*, 7.

28. Christopher Wlezien, "The Public as Thermostat: Dynamics of Preferences for Spending." *American Journal of Political Science* 39, no. 4 (1995), 981–1000.

29. The question appeared on the General Social Survey in all years from 1973 to 1994, except 1979, 1981, and 1992. From 1994 to 2010, the question was asked only in even-numbered years. The data and codebook are available from the General

Social Survey website, http://www3.norc.org/GSS+Website/. In combining responses for years in which the wording of the question varied slightly, we followed Dunlap and Scarce, "Poll Trends." In computing the variable as net support for more spending on the environment, we followed Wlezien, "Patterns of Representation." We experimented with lagging the public opinion data by one to three years in regression models. In computing annual percent change in polling data for inclusion in regression models, we interpolated to estimate values for missing years. We also interpolated to estimate values for missing years in presenting the time trends in Figures 5.2 and 5.4.

30. The Cambridge data are from Dunlap and Scarce, "Poll Trends," and include all years from 1976 to 1990, with the exception of 1980. The Gallup data are from Gallup, "Environment," and include all years from 1991 to 2010, except 1993, 1994, and 1996. We experimented with lagging the public opinion data by one to three years in regression models. In computing annual percent change in polling data for inclusion in regression models, we interpolated to estimate values for missing years. We also interpolated to estimate values for missing years in presenting the time trends in Figures 5.2 and 5.4.

31. Pearson correlation coefficient (two-tailed) for the two polling measures through 1998 = 0.81, $p < 0.001$, calculated with actual data only, omitting interpolated values.

32. $N = 38$, the years from 1973 to 2010, inclusive. The sample sizes are lower when including lagged values for the polling data because of missing data in the early years.

33. OLS results, $p > 0.1$ for all tested political and economic variables (unlagged or lagged, including interaction terms) and for public opinion polling data (lagged zero, one, or two years, from both surveys). The regression equation for the bivariate model with General Social Survey data lagged three years (GSS $t - 3$), is: $\hat{y} = 1.12 + 0.39^*(GSS\ t - 3)$. Standard errors = 1.48 for the constant and 0.18 for the GSS coefficient ($p = 0.04$). $R^2 = 0.13$. Standard error of estimate = 8.61. $N = 34$.

34. Agnone, "Amplifying Public Opinion"; Wlezien, "Patterns of Representation."

35. Robert Higgs and Anthony Kilduff, "Public Opinion: A Powerful Predictor of U.S. Defense Spending." *Defence Economics* 4, no. 3 (1993), 227–238.

36. For the General Social Survey polling data lagged three years, the Pearson correlation coefficient (two-tailed) for the bivariate relationship with the EPA budget data = 0.73 ($p < 0.001$); for the Cambridge/Gallup data lagged three years, the correlation with the EPA budget data = 0.67 ($p = 0.003$). In both cases, the correlations are calculated with actual polling data omitting interpolated values.

37. Pearson correlation coefficient (two-tailed) = 0.72 ($p < 0.001$).

38. To avoid distortions from the startup period of rapid growth, we omit 1971 and 1972.

39. For discussion of budgetary competition between the president and Congress, see, for instance, Kiewiet and McCubbins, "Appropriations Decisions"; D. Roderick Kiewiet and Mathew D. McCubbins, "Presidential Influence on Congressional Appropriations Decisions." *American Journal of Political Science* 32, no. 3 (1988), 713–736; Christopher Wlezien and Stuart N. Soroka, "Measures and Models

of Budgetary Policy." *Policy Studies Journal* 31 no. 2 (2003), 273–286; Brandice Canes-Wrone, William G. Howell, and David E. Lewis, "Toward a Broader Understanding of Presidential Power: A Reevaluation of the Two Presidencies Thesis." *Journal of Politics* 70, no. 1 (2008), 1–16.

40. Figure 5.6 presents data for the thirty-nine years from 1972 to 2010, inclusive. The president did not make official budget proposals for the EPA in FY 1970 or 1971 because the agency was not formally established until December 1970, when FY 1971 was already under way.

41. As we discuss in detail below, the gap in 1982 is deceptive. The incoming Reagan administration engineered the large cut in the EPA's budget through a legislative mechanism.

42. Ruckelshaus, "Stopping the Pendulum."

43. For instance, Marc K. Landy, Marc J. Roberts, and Stephen R. Thomas, *The Environmental Protection Agency* (New York: Oxford University Press, 1994); Michael E. Kraft, *Environmental Policy and Politics*, 5th ed. (Boston, MA: Longman, 2011).

44. John William Ellwood, "Congress Cuts the Budget: The Omnibus Reconciliation Act of 1981." *Public Budgeting & Finance* 2, no. 1 (1982): 50–64.

45. *Ibid.*, 50.

46. Government Accountability Office, *A Glossary of Terms Used in the Federal Budget Process* (Washington, D.C.: Government Printing Office, 2005).

47. Walter A. Rosenbaum, "Science, Politics, and Policy at the EPA," in *Environmental Policy*, 8th ed., ed. Norman J. Vig and Michael E. Kraft (Thousand Oaks, CA: CQ Press, 2013), 158–184.

48. Ruckelshaus, " Stopping the Pendulum," 229.

49. *Ibid.*, 229.

CHAPTER 6

1. John William Ellwood, "Congress Cuts the Budget: The Omnibus Reconciliation Act of 1981." *Public Budgeting & Finance* 2, no. 1 (1982): 50–64.

2. Caldwell and Bear describe Clinton's proposed bureaucratic realignment as representing a clear misreading of NEPA requirements and a profound misunderstanding of the CEQ's statutory purpose. L.K. Caldwell, "Environmental Policy and NEPA: Past, Present, and Future," in *Environmental Policy and NEPA: Past, Present, and Future*, ed. E. Ray Clark and Larry W. Canter (Boca Raton, FL: St. Lucie Press, 1997), 37 and 34. Dinah Bear, "The National Environmental Policy Act: Its Origins and Evolutions." *Natural Resources and Environment* 10 no. 2 (1995), 3–6, 69–73.

3. James Q. Wilson, *Bureaucracy: What Government Agencies Do and Why They Do It* (Basic Books: 2000), xix.

4. *Ibid.*

5. *Ibid.*

6. Anthony Downs, "Up and Down with Ecology—The Issue Attention Cycle." *Public Interest*, 28 (1972: Summer), 38–50.

7. Milo Mason, "Interview: James L. Connaughton." *Natural Resources and Environment* 23 no. 2 (2008), 36–39.

8. Anthony Downs, *Inside Bureaucracy* (Boston: Little Brown, 1967), 9.

9. *Ibid.*

10. *Ibid.*, 10.

11. Useful background information on the Executive Office of the President can be found in Harold C. Relaya, "The Executive Office of the President: An Historical Overview," CRS Report for Congress, updated November 2008. https://www.fas.org/sgp/crs/misc/98-606.pdf.

12. For example, Gerald Auten, Barry Bozeman, and Robert Cline, "A Sequential Model of Congressional Appropriations." *American Journal of Political Science* 28, no. 3 (1984), 503–523.

13. Ibid.

14. This decision deserves some explanation. As reported in our summary and analysis of the biological model in Chapter 3, Downs takes the position that "exogenous factors," particularly interest groups and Congress, will ultimately determine whether an agency survives or prospers. Yet, Downs also identifies "internal" or agency-related factors, including the leadership, size, and age of the agency, as key factors that determine an agency's survival and prosperity. Given this seeming contradiction, and given the way we think the variables should be listed in our three-variable cluster framework (Table 6.2), we decided not to classify the biological model as a model in which "external" factors are the dominant independent variables.

15. Kettl, *The Politics of the Administrative Process*, 5th ed. (Washington, D.C.: CQ Press, 2012), 135.

CHAPTER 7

1. Nate Silver, *The Signal and the Noise: Why So Many Predictions Fail—But Some Don't* (New York: Penguin, 2012).

2. Phillip E. Tetlock, *Expert Political Judgment: How Good Is It? How Can We Know?* (Princeton, NJ: Princeton University Press, 2006), 81.

3. Intergovernmental Panel on Climate Change, "Summary for Policymakers," in *Climate Change 2014: Impacts, Adaptation, and Vulnerability. Part A: Global and Sectoral Aspects. Contribution of Working Group II to the Fifth Assessment Report of the Intergovernmental Panel on Climate Change* (Cambridge, UK: Cambridge University Press, 2014), http://www.ipcc.ch/report/ar5/wg2/.

4. In offering predictions as thought exercises, we follow the example of geographer Laurence C. Smith, who used this approach in his book *The World in 2050: Four Forces Shaping Civilization's Northern Future* (New York: Dutton, 2010).

5. Daniel P. Carpenter and David E. Lewis, "Political Learning from Rare Events: Poisson Inference, Fiscal Constraints, and the Lifetime of Bureaus." *Political Analysis* 12, no. 3 (2004), 201–232.

6. Russell E. Train, *Politics, Pollution, and Pandas: An Environmental Memoir* (Washington, D.C.: Shearwater, 2003).

7. John M. Broder, "Bashing E.P.A. Is New Theme in G.O.P. Race." *New York Times*, August 18, 2011, http://www.nytimes.com/2011/08/18/us/politics/18epa.html.

8. Anthony Adragna, "Republicans Plan to Attack over EPA Rules in Fall Elections." *Bloomberg*, June 5, 2014, http://www.bloomberg.com/news/2014-06-05/republicans-plan-to-attack-over-epa-rules-in-fall-elections.html.

9. Herbert Kaufman, *Are Government Organizations Immortal?* (Washington, D.C.: Brookings, 1976).

10. Carpenter and Lewis, "Political Learning." See also David E. Lewis, "The Politics of Agency Termination: Confronting the Myth of Agency Immortality." *Journal of Politics* 61, no. 1 (2002), 89–107.

11. Lou Cannon and Carl M. Canon, *Reagan's Disciple* (New York: Public Affairs, 2005), 60.

12. $P = 0.2*0.45*0.6*0.2 = 0.011$. We acknowledge the many limitations of these crude calculations but believe a rough quantitative estimate may have some value over political instincts.

13. The binomial probability $P(x = 1)$, with four trials and a probability of success in a given trial of 0.011 (see footnote 12), is 0.043. The possibility of the EPA being eliminated more than once in the time period is not relevant. We acknowledge the many limitations of this rough estimate, including that nominating cycles are not independent trials.

14. Census Bureau, "U.S. Census Bureau Projections Show a Slower Growing, Older, More Diverse Nation a Half Century from Now," News Release, December 12, 2012, http://www.census.gov/newsroom/releases/archives/population/cb12-243.html.

15. John Judis and Ruy Teixeira, *The Emerging Democratic Majority* (New York: Scribner, 2002); and Ruy Teixeira, ed., *Red, Blue and Purple America: The Future of Election Demographics* (Washington, D.C.: Brookings, 2008).

16. Daniel J. Fiorino, *The New Environmental Regulation* (Cambridge, MA: MIT Press, 2006).

17. Environmental Protection Agency, *The Benefits and Costs of the Clean Air Act, 1970 to 1990*, October 1997, http://www.epa.gov/cleanairactbenefits/copy.html.

18. Council of Economic Advisors, *2012 Economic Report of the President* (Washington, D.C.: Government Printing Office, 2012), http://www.whitehouse.gov/sites/default/files/microsites/ERP_2012_Complete.pdf.

19. Robert W. Hahn and Gordon L. Hester, "Marketable Permits: Lessons for Theory and Practice." *Ecology Law Quarterly* 16 (1989): 361–406.

20. A. Denny Ellerman, Paul L. Joskow, Richard Schmalensee, Juan-Pablo Montero, and Elizabeth M. Bailey, *Markets for Clean Air: The U.S. Acid Rain Program* (Cambridge, UK: Cambridge University Press, 2000); Richard Schmalensee and Robert N. Stavins, *The SO_2 Allowance Trading System: The Ironic History of a Grand Policy Experiment* (Cambridge, MA: MIT Center for Energy and Environmental Policy Research, 2012), http://web.mit.edu/ceepr/www/publications/workingpapers/2012-012.pdf.

21. Fiorino, *New Environmental Regulation*.

22. William Nordhaus, *The Climate Casino: Risk, Uncertainty, and Economics for a Warming World* (New Haven, CT: Yale University Press, 2013).

23. Michael E. Kraft, *Environmental Policy and Politics*, 5th ed. (Boston, MA: Longman, 2012).

24. Corey Davenport, "Climate Campaign Can't Be Deaf to Economic Worries, Obama Warns." *New York Times*, June 26, 2014, http://www.nytimes.com/2014/06/26/us/politics/obama-warns-climate-campaign-cant-be-deaf-to-economic-worries.html.

25. Dinah Bear, Ray Clark, William M. Cohen, Mark S. Davis, Michael R. Deland, Robert Dreher, George Frampton, Oliver A. Houck, Thomas C. Jensen, Nathaniel S.W. Lawrence, Kathleen McGinty, Roger Schlickeisen, James Gustav Speth, David Struhs, James Strock, Russel E. Train, James T.B. Tripp, Brook B. Yeager, and Nicholas C. Yost. *Facing the Future: Recommendations on the White House Council on Environmental Quality—A Report to the President-Elect* (New Orleans, LA: Tulane Institute on Water Resources Law and Policy, Tulane Law School, 2008).

26. William D. Ruckelshaus, "Stopping the Pendulum." *Environmental Toxicology and Chemistry* 15, no. 3 (1996), 229.

27. Quoted in Carpenter and Lewis, "Political Learning," 206.

28. National Environmental Policy Act of 1969 (P.L. 91–190, 42 U.S.C 4321–47, January 1, 1970), http://ceq.hss.doe.gov/nepa/regs/nepa/nepaeqia.htm.

POSTSCRIPT

1. National Environmental Policy Act of 1969 (P.L. 91–190). The full text of the law is presented in Appendix 1.

2. United Nations World Commission on Environment and Development, *Our Common Future* (New York: Oxford University Press, 1987).

3. Paul Gilman, "New EPA Focus on Sustainability," *Science* 304, no. 5675 (2004): 1243–1247.

4. National Research Council, *Sustainability and the U.S. EPA* (Washington, D.C.: The National Academies Press, 2011), http://www.nap.edu/catalog/13152/sustainability-and-the-us-epa.

5. See, for example, Joop F.M. Koppenjan and Bert Enserink, "Public-Private Partnerships in Urban Infrastructures: Reconciling Private Sector Participation and Sustainability." *Public Administration Review* 69, no. 2 (2009): 284–296; Michael A. Berry and Dennis A. Rondinelli, "Proactive Corporate Environmental Management: A New Industrial Revolution." *Academy of Management Perspectives* 12, no. 2 (1998): 38–50.

6. For summary and details of climate change science and policy, see the *Fifth Assessment Report* of the Intergovernmental Panel on Climate Change, released in 2014 and 2015, http://www.ipcc.ch.

7. International Energy Agency, 2014 Key World Energy Statistics, http://www.iea.org/publications/freepublications/publication/keyworld2014.pdf.

8. International Energy Agency, 2014 CO_2 Emissions from Fuel Combustion, https://www.iea.org/publications/freepublications/publication/CO2EmissionsFromFuelCombustionHighlights2014.pdf.

9. Environmental Protection Agency, "Climate Change Indicators," http://www.epa.gov/climatechange/science/indicators/weather-climate/temperature.html.

10. Intergovernmental Panel on Climate Change, *Climate Change 2014 Synthesis Report Summary for Policymakers*, http://www.ipcc.ch/pdf/assessment-report/ar5/syr/AR5_SYR_FINAL_SPM.pdf.

11. US Energy Information Administration, "Frequently Asked Questions," http://www.eia.gov/tools/faqs/faq.cfm?id=73&t=11.

12. Environmental Protection Agency, "EPA and NHTSA Set Standards to Reduce Greenhouse Gases and Improve Fuel Economy for Model Years 2017–2025 Cars and Light Trucks," EPA-420-F-12-051, August 2012, http://www.epa.gov/otaq/climate/documents/420f12051.pdf.

13. Environmental Protection Agency, "Voluntary Energy and Climate Programs," http://www.epa.gov/climatechange/EPAactivities/voluntaryprograms.html.

14. Environmental Protection Agency, "What is EPA Doing about Climate Change?" http://www.epa.gov/climatechange/EPAactivities.html.

15. Environmental Protection Agency, "Clean Power Plan Proposed Rule," http://www2.epa.gov/carbon-pollution-standards/clean-power-plan-proposed-rule. The EPA previously proposed standards for new power plants, initially releasing standards for new sources in 2012 and then replacing them with revised standards in 2013 in response to public comments.

16. Environmental Protection Agency, "EPA Fact Sheet: Clean Power Plan National Framework for States," http://www2.epa.gov/sites/production/files/2014-05/documents/20140602fs-overview.pdf.

17. See for example, Charles T. Driscoll, Jonathan J. Buonocore, Jonathan I. Levy, Kathleen F. Lambert, Dallas Burtraw, Stephen B. Reid, Habibollah Fakhraei, and Joel Schwartz, "US Power Plant Carbon Standards and Clean Air and Health Co-Benefits," *Nature Climate Change*, published online May 4, 2015, DOI: 10.1038/Nclimate2598; Janneke Hille Ris Lambers, "Extinction Risks from Climate Change: How Will Climate Change Affect Global Biodiversity?" *Science* 348, no. 6234 (2015): 501–502.

18. Environmental Protection Agency, *Regulatory Impact Analysis for the Proposed Carbon Pollution Guidelines for Existing Power Plants and Emission Standards for Modified and Reconstructed Power Plants*, ES–20, EPA-452/R-14-002, June 2014, http://www2.epa.gov/sites/production/files/2014-06/documents/20140602ria-clean-power-plan.pdf.

19. Coral Davenport, "McConnell Urges States to Help Thwart Obama's 'War on Coal.'" *New York Times*, March 20, 2015, http://www.nytimes.com/2015/03/20/us/politics/mitch-mcconnell-urges-states-to-help-thwart-obamas-war-on-coal.html?_r=0.

APPENDIX 2

1. *The U.S. Government Manual 2012–2013* (Washington, D.C.: U.S. Government Printing Office, 2013).

2. Harold C. Relaya, "The Executive Office of the President: An Historical Overview," CRS Report for Congress, updated November 2008, https://www.fas.org/sgp/crs/misc/98-606.pdf

3. *Ibid.*

4. Donald F. Kettl, *The Politics of the Administrative Process*, 5th ed. (Washington, D.C.: CQ Press, 2012) p. 135. State and Treasury are the oldest departments (1789); Homeland Security is the newest (2002). Education was the smallest Cabinet department in FY 2012, with approximately 4,500 employees; Defense was the largest, with approximately 748,000 employees. Health and Human Services had the largest spending total in FY 2012, with outlays of $893 million; Interior had the smallest total, with outlays of $13.8 million.

BIBLIOGRAPHY

Adragna, Anthony. "Republicans Plan to Attack over EPA Rules in Fall Elections." *Bloomberg*, June 5, 2014, http://www.bloomberg.com/news/2014-06-05/republicans-plan-to-attack-over-epa-rules-in-fall-elections.html.

Agnone, Jon. "Amplifying Public Opinion: The Policy Impact of the U.S. Environmental Movement." *Social Forces* 85, no. 4 (2007): 1593–1620.

Anderson, Frederick R. *NEPA in the Courts: A Legal Analysis of the National Environmental Policy Act.* Washington, D.C.: Resources for the Future Press, 1973.

Auten, Gerald, Barry Bozeman, and Robert Cline. "A Sequential Model of Congressional Appropriations." *American Journal of Political Science* 28, no. 3 (1984): 503–523.

Balint, Peter J., and James K. Conant. "The Environmental Protection Agency's Budget from 1970–2010: A Life cycle Analysis." *Public Budgeting and Finance* 33, no 4 (2013): 22–42.

Balint, Peter J., Ronald E. Stewart, Anand Desai, and Lawrence C. Walters. *Wicked Environmental Problems: Managing Uncertainty and Conflict.* Washington, D.C.: Island Press, 2011.

Bear, Dinah. "The National Environmental Policy Act: Its Origins and Evolutions." *Natural Resources and Environment* 10, no. 2 (1995): 3–6, 69–73.

Bear, Dinah, Ray Clark, William M. Cohen, Mark S. Davis, Michael R. Deland, Robert Dreher, George Frampton, Oliver A. Houck, Thomas C. Jensen, Nathaniel S.W. Lawrence, Kathleen McGinty, Roger Schlickeisen, James Gustave Speth, David Struhs, James Strock, Russell E. Train, James T.B. Tripp, Brooks B. Yeager, and Nicholas C. Yost. "Facing the Future: Recommendations on the White House Council on Environmental Quality—A Report to the President-Elect." Tulane Law School, New Orleans, LA: Tulane Institute on Water Resources Law and Policy, 2008, http://www.law.tulane.edu/uploadedFiles/Institutes_and_Centers/Water_Resources_Law_and_Policy/Documents/Facing%20the%20Future.pdf.

Berry, Michael A., and Dennis A. Rondinelli. "Proactive Corporate Environmental Management: A New Industrial Revolution." *Academy of Management Perspectives* 12, no. 2 (1998): 38–50.

Bozeman, Barry. "The Effect of Economic and Partisan Change on Federal Appropriations." *Western Political Quarterly* 30, no. 1 (1977): 112–224.

Braybrooke, David, and Charles E. Lindblom. *A Strategy of Decision: Policy Evaluation as Social Process*. New York: The Free Press, 1963.

Broder, John M. "Bashing E.P.A. Is New Theme in G.O.P. Race." *New York Times*, August 18, 2011, http://www.nytimes.com/2011/08/18/us/politics/18epa.html.

Bureau of Economic Analysis. "Gross Domestic Product Tables," http://www.bea.gov.

Bureau of Labor Statistics. "Unemployment Tables," http://www.bls.gov/data/#unemployment.

Bush, George H.W. *Address Accepting the Presidential Nomination*, Republican National Convention, New Orleans, August 18, 1988, http://www.presidency.ucsb.edu/ws/?pid=25955.

Caldwell, Lynton K. "Implementing NEPA: A Non-Technical Political Task," in *Environmental Policy and NEPA: Past, Present, and Future*, ed. E. Ray Clark and Larry W. Canter. Boca Raton, FL: St. Lucie Press, 1997, 25–50.

Caldwell, Lynton K. *The National Environmental Policy Act: An Agenda for the Future*. Bloomington: Indiana University Press, 1998.

Canes-Wrone, Brandice, William G. Howell, and David E. Lewis. "Toward a Broader Understanding of Presidential Power: A Reevaluation of the Two Presidencies Thesis." *Journal of Politics* 70, no. 1 (2008): 1–16.

Cannon, Lou, and Carl M. Canon. *Reagan's Disciple*. New York: Public Affairs, 2005.

Carcasson, Martin. "Prudence, Procrastination, or Politics: George Bush and the Earth Summit of 1992," in *The Rhetorical Presidency of George H. W. Bush*, ed. Marin J. Medhurst. College Station: Texas A&M University Press, 2006, 119–148.

Carpenter, Daniel P. "Stochastic Prediction and Estimation of Nonlinear Political Durations: An Application to the Lifetime of Bureaus," in *Political Complexity: Nonlinear Models of Politics*, ed. D. Richards. Ann Arbor: University of Michigan Press, 2000, 209–238.

Carpenter, Daniel P., and David E. Lewis. "Political Learning from Rare Events: Poisson Inference, Fiscal Constraints, and the Lifetime of Bureaus." *Political Analysis* 12, no. 3 (2004): 201–232.

Carson, Rachel. *Silent Spring*. Boston, MA: Houghton Mifflin, 1962.

Census Bureau. "U.S. Census Bureau Projections Show a Slower Growing, Older, More Diverse Nation a Half Century from Now." News Release, December 12, 2012, http://www.census.gov/newsroom/releases/archives/population/cb12-243.html.

Chesnut, Louraine G., and David M. Mills. "A Fresh Look at the Benefits and Costs of the US Acid Rain Program." *Journal of Environmental Management* 77, no. 3 (2005): 252–266.

Clark, E. Ray, and Larry W. Canter, eds. *Environmental Policy and NEPA: Past, Present, and Future*. Boca Raton, FL: St. Lucie Press, 1997.

Clarke, Keith C., and Jeffrey J. Hemphill. "The Santa Barbara Oil Spill, A Retrospective," in *Yearbook of the Association of Pacific Coast Geographers, Vol. 64*, ed. Darrick Danta. Honolulu: University of Hawai'i Press, 2002, 157–162, http://www.geog.ucsb.edu/~kclarke/Papers/SBOilSpill1969.pdf.

Conant, James K. "The Changing Face of the New Jersey Department of Environmental Protection." *The Environmental Forum* 4, no. 8 (1985): 45–53.

Conant, James K. "Stability, Change and Leadership in State Administration: 1970–1986." *State and Local Government Review* 21, no. 1 (1989): 3–10.

Conant, James K., and Peter J. Balint. "The Council on Environmental Quality at 40: A Life Cycle Analysis." *Environmental Practice* 13, no. 2 (2011): 113–121.

Congressional Budget Office, "Historical Budget Data," http://www.cbo.gov/publication/21999.

Council of Economic Advisors. *2012 Economic Report of the President.* Washington, D.C.: Government Printing Office, 2012, http://www.whitehouse.gov/sites/default/files/microsites/ERP_2012_Complete.pdf.

Council on Environmental Quality. *Environmental Quality: The First Annual Report of the Council on Environmental Quality.* Washington, D.C.: U.S. Government Printing Office, 1970.

Council on Environmental Quality. *The Global 2000 Report to the President: Entering the Twenty-First Century.* Washington, D.C.: U.S. Government Printing Office, 1980.

Davenport, Coral. "Climate Campaign Can't Be Deaf to Economic Worries, Obama Warns." *New York Times*, June 26, 2014, http://www.nytimes.com/2014/06/26/us/politics/obama-warns-climate-campaign-cant-be-deaf-to-economic-worries.html.

Davenport, Coral. "McConnell Urges States to Help Thwart Obama's 'War on Coal.'" *New York Times*, March 20, 2015, http://www.nytimes.com/2015/03/20/us/politics/mitch-mcconnell-urges-states-to-help-thwart-obamas-war-on-coal.html?_r=0

Davis, Otto A., M.A.H. Dempster, and Aaron Wildavsky. "The Politics of the Budgetary Process." *American Political Science Review* 60, no. 3 (1966): 529–547.

Dempster, M.A.H., Aaron Wildavsky, and Otto A. Davis. "Toward a Predictive Theory of Government Expenditure: US Domestic Appropriations." *British Journal of Political Science* 4, no. 4 (1974): 419–452.

Dinda, Soumyananda. "Environmental Kuznets Curve Hypothesis: A Survey." *Ecological Economics* 49, no. 4 (2004): 431–455.

Downs, Anthony. *Inside Bureaucracy.* Boston, MA: Little Brown, 1967.

Downs, Anthony. "Up and Down with Ecology—The 'Issue-Attention Cycle.'" *Public Interest* 28 (1972): 38–50.

Driscoll, Charles T., Jonathan J. Buonocore, Jonathan I. Levy, Kathleen F. Lambert, Dallas Burtraw, Stephen B. Reid, Habibollah Fakhraei, and Joel Schwartz. "US Power Plant Carbon Standards and Clean Air and Health Co-Benefits," *Nature Climate Change*, published online May 4, 2015, DOI: 10.1038/Nclimate2598.

Drucker, Peter F. *The Age of Discontinuity: Guidelines to Our Changing Society.* London: Heinemann, 1969.

Dunlap, Riley E., and Rik Scarce. "Poll Trends: Environmental Problems and Protection." *Public Opinion Quarterly* 55, no. 4 (1991): 651–672.

Ellerman, A. Denny, Paul L. Joskow, Richard Schmalensee, Juan-Pablo Montero, and Elizabeth M. Bailey. *Markets for Clean Air: The U.S. Acid Rain Program.* Cambridge, UK: Cambridge University Press, 2000.

Ellwood, John William. "Congress Cuts the Budget: The Omnibus Reconciliation Act of 1981." *Public Budgeting & Finance* 2, no. 1 (1982): 50–64.

Energy Information Administration. "Frequently Asked Questions," http://www.eia.gov/tools/faqs/faq.cfm?id=73&t=11.

Environmental Protection Agency. "Air Quality Trends," http://www.epa.gov/airtrends/aqtrends.html#comparison.

Environmental Protection Agency. *The Benefits and Costs of the Clean Air Act, 1970 to 1990*, October 1997, http://www.epa.gov/cleanairactbenefits/copy.html.

Environmental Protection Agency. "Clean Power Plan Proposed Rule," http://www2.epa.gov/carbon-pollution-standards/clean-power-plan-proposed-rule.

Environmental Protection Agency. "Climate Change Indicators," http://www.epa.gov/climatechange/science/indicators/weather-climate/temperature.html.

Environmental Protection Agency. "EPA and NHTSA Set Standards to Reduce Greenhouse Gases and Improve Fuel Economy for Model Years 2017–2025 Cars and Light Trucks," EPA-420-F-12-051, August 2012, http://www.epa.gov/otaq/climate/documents/420f12051.pdf.

Environmental Protection Agency. "EPA Fact Sheet: Clean Power Plan National Framework for States," http://www2.epa.gov/sites/production/files/2014-05/documents/20140602fs-overview.pdf.

Environmental Protection Agency. "Executive Summary," in *The Benefits and Costs of the Clean Air Act, 1970 to 1990*, October 1997, http://www.epa.gov/air/sect812/1970-1990/812exec2.pdf.

Environmental Protection Agency. "Fact Sheet: EPA's Revised Particulate Matter Standards." July 17, 1997, http://www.epa.gov/ttn/oarpg/t1/fact_sheets/pmfact.pdf.

Environmental Protection Agency. *National Summary of State Information*, "Watershed Assessment, Tracking & Environmental Results," http://ofmpub.epa.gov/waters10/attains_nation_cy.control#prob_surv_states.

Environmental Protection Agency. *Regulatory Impact Analysis for the Proposed Carbon Pollution Guidelines for Existing Power Plants and Emission Standards for Modified and Reconstructed Power Plants*, ES-20, EPA-452/R-14-002, June 2014, http://www2.epa.gov/sites/production/files/2014–06/documents/20140602ria-clean-power-plan.pdf.

Environmental Protection Agency. "Six Common Pollutants," http://www.epa.gov/air/urbanair/.

Environmental Protection Agency. "Voluntary Energy and Climate Programs," http://www.epa.gov/climatechange/EPAactivities/voluntaryprograms.html.

Environmental Protection Agency. "What is EPA Doing about Climate Change?" http://www.epa.gov/climatechange/EPAactivities.html.

Fiorino, Daniel J. *The New Environmental Regulation*. Cambridge, MA: MIT Press, 2006.

Freeman III, A. Myrick. "Environmental Policy Since Earth Day I: What Have We Gained?" *Journal of Economic Perspectives* 16, no. 1 (2002): 125–146.

Gallup. "Environment," August 5, 2014, http://www.gallup.com/poll/1615/environment.aspx#1.

Gawthrop, Louis C. *Public Service and Democracy: Ethical Imperatives for the 21st Century*. New York: Chatham House, 1998.

General Social Survey. http://www3.norc.org/GSS+Website/.

Gilman, Paul. "New EPA Focus on Sustainability." *Science* 304, no. 5675 (2004): 1243–1247.

Government Accountability Office. *A Glossary of Terms Used in the Federal Budget Process*. Washington, D.C.: U.S. Government Printing Office, 2005.

Government Accounting Office. Report of the Comptroller General of the United States. "The Council on Environmental Quality: A Tool for Shaping National Policy." CEC-81-66, March 19, 1981, http://www.gao.gov/assets/140/132363.pdf.

Hahn, Robert W., and Gordon L. Hester. "Marketable Permits: Lessons for Theory and Practice." *Ecology Law Quarterly* 16 (1989): 361–406.

Heith, Diane J. *Polling to Govern: Public Opinion and Presidential Leadership*. Stanford, CA: Stanford University Press, 2004.

Higgs, Robert, and Anthony Kilduff. "Public Opinion: A Powerful Predictor of U.S. Defense Spending." *Defence Economics* 4, no. 3 (1993): 227–238.

Intergovernmental Panel on Climate Change. "Summary for Policymakers," in *Climate Change 2014: Impacts, Adaptation, and Vulnerability. Part A: Global and Sectoral Aspects. Contribution of Working Group II to the Fifth Assessment Report of the Intergovernmental Panel on Climate Change*. Cambridge, UK: Cambridge University Press, 2014, http://www.ipcc.ch/report/ar5/wg2/.

International Energy Agency. *2014 CO_2 Emissions from Fuel Combustion*, https://www.iea.org/publications/freepublications/publication/CO$_2$EmissionsFromFuelCombustionHighlights2014.pdf.

International Energy Agency. *2014 Key World Energy Statistics*, http://www.iea.org/publications/freepublications/publication/keyworld2014.pdf.

Judis, John, and Ruy Teixeira. *The Emerging Democratic Majority*. New York: Scribner, 2002.

Kaufman, Herbert. *Are Government Organizations Immortal?* Washington, D.C.: Brookings, 1976.

Kaufman, Herbert. *The Limits of Organizational Change*. Tuscaloosa: University of Alabama Press, 1972.

Kiewiet, D. Roderick, and Mathew D. McCubbins. "Appropriations Decisions as a Bilateral Bargaining Game between President and Congress." *Legislative Studies Quarterly* 10, no. 2 (1985): 181–201.

Kiewiet, D. Roderick, and Mathew D. McCubbins. "Presidential Influence on Congressional Appropriations Decisions." *American Journal of Political Science* 32, no. 3 (1988): 713–736.

Kohut, Andrew. "But What Do the Polls Show," in *The Politics of News: The News of Politics*, 2nd ed., ed. Doris A. Graber, Dennis McQuail, and Pippa Norris. Washington, D.C.: CQ Press, 2008, 190–210.

Koppenjan, Joop F.M., and Bert Enserink. "Public-Private Partnerships in Urban Infrastructures: Reconciling Private Sector Participation and Sustainability." *Public Administration Review* 69, no. 2 (2009): 284–296.

Kraft, Michael E. *Environmental Policy and Politics*, 5th ed. Boston: Longman, 2011.

Kraft, Michael E. "Environmental Policy in Congress," in *Environmental Policy: New Directions for the Twenty-First Century*, 8th ed., ed. Norman J. Vig and Michael E. Kraft. Thousand Oaks, CA: CQ Press, 2013, 109–134.

Kraft, Michael E., and Norman J. Vig. "Environmental Policy over Four Decades," in *Environmental Policy: New Directions for the Twenty-First Century*, 8th ed., ed. Norman J. Vig and Michael E. Kraft. Thousand Oaks, CA: CQ Press, 2013, 2–29.

Lambers, Janneke Hille Ris. "Extinction Risks from Climate Change: How Will Climate Change Affect Global Biodiversity?" *Science* 348, no. 6234 (2015): 501–502.

Landy, Marc K., Marc J. Roberts, and Stephen R. Thomas. *The Environmental Protection Agency*. New York: Oxford University Press, 1994.

Lewis, David E. "The Politics of Agency Termination: Confronting the Myth of Agency Immortality." *Journal of Politics* 61, no. 1 (2002): 89–107.

Lewis, Jack. "The Birth of the EPA." *EPA Journal* (November 1985), http://www2.epa.gov/aboutepa/birth-epa.

Lilienthal, David E. *TVA—Democracy on the March*, 2nd ed. New York: Harper, 1953.

Lindblom, Charles E. *The Intelligence of Democracy: Decision Making through Mutual Adjustments*. New York: Free Press, 1965.

Lindblom, Charles E. "The Science of 'Muddling Through.'" *Public Administration Review* 19, no. 2 (1959): 79–88.

Lindstrom, Matthew J., and Zachary A. Smith. *The National Environmental Policy Act*. College Station: Texas A&M University Press, 2001.

MacLeish, Archibald. "Riders on Earth Together, Brothers in Eternal Cold." *New York Times*, December 25, 1968, http://www.nytimes.com/2008/12/24/opinion/24wed4.html?emc=etal.

Malakoff, David. "The Gas Surge." *Science* 344, no. 6191 (2014): 1464–1467.

Mason, Milo. "Interview: James L Connaughton." *Natural Resources & Environment* 23, no. 2 (2008): 36–39.

National Archives and Records Administration. "Act creating Yellowstone National Park," March 1, 1872": Enrolled Acts and Resolutions of Congress, 1789–1996; General Records of the United States Government; Record Group 11; National Archives, http://www.ourdocuments.gov/doc.php?doc=45.

National Environmental Policy Act of 1969 (P.L. 91–190). [The full text of the law is presented in Appendix 1.]

National Research Council. *Achieving Nutrient and Sediment Reduction Goals in the Chesapeake Bay: An Evaluation of Program Strategies and Implementation*. Washington, D.C.: The National Academies Press, 2011.

National Research Council. *Sustainability and the U.S. EPA*. Washington, D.C.: The National Academies Press, 2011.

Nixon, Richard M. "Annual Message to the Congress on the State of the Union," January 22, 1970, http://www.presidency.ucsb.edu/ws/?pid=2921.

Nixon, Richard M. "Special Message to the Congress about Reorganization Plans to Establish the Environmental Protection Agency and the National Oceanic and Atmospheric Administraton," July 9, 1970, in *Public Papers of the Presidents of the United States: Richard M. Nixon 1970*. Washington, D.C.: U.S. Government Printing Office, 1971, 578–586, http://quod.lib.umich.edu/p/ppotpus/4731750.1970.001?view=toc.

Nixon, Richard M. "Title 5, Appendix—Reorganization Plan No. 3 of 1970." July 9, 1970. Washington, D.C.: U.S. Government Printing Office, 1971, 202–207, http://www.gpo.gov/fdsys/pkg/USCODE-2011-title5/pdf/USCODE-2011-title5-app-reorganiz-other-dup92.pdf.

Nordhaus, William. *The Climate Casino: Risk, Uncertainty, and Economics for a Warming World*. New Haven, CT: Yale University Press, 2013.

Office of Management and Budget. *Budget of the United States Government*, Federal Reserve Archives, http://fraser.stlouisfed.org/publication/?pid=54.

Portney, Paul R. "Air Pollution Policy," in *Public Policies for Environmental Protection*, 2nd ed., ed. Paul R. Portney and Robert N. Stavins. Washington, DC: Resources for the Future, 2000, 77–124.

Reagan, Ronald. *Inaugural Address*, January 20, 1981, http://www.presidency.ucsb.edu/ws/?pid=43130.

Remnick, David. "Ozone Man." *New Yorker*. April 24, 2006, http://www.newyorker.com/archive/2006/04/24/060424ta_talk_remnick.

Revkin, Andrew A., and Matthew L. Wald. "Former Bush White House Aide Defends Edits to Global Warming Reports." *New York Times*, March 20, 2007, http://www.nytimes.com/2007/03/20/world/americas/20iht-climate.4966561.html.

Robinson, Nicholas A. "NEPA at 40: International Dimensions." Pace Law Faculty Publications, Paper 575 (2009), http://digitalcommons.pace.edu/lawfaculty/575.

Rosenbaum, Walter A. *Environmental Politics and Policy*, 9th ed. Washington, D.C.: CQ Press, 2013.

Rosenbaum, Walter A. "Science, Politics, and Policy at the EPA," in *Environmental Policy: New Directions for the Twenty-First Century*, 8th ed., ed. Norman J. Vig and Michael E. Kraft. Thousand Oaks, CA: CQ Press, 2013, 158–184.

Ruckelshaus, William D. "Stopping the Pendulum." *Environmental Toxicology and Chemistry* 15, no. 3 (1996): 229–232.

Scheberle, Denise. *Federalism and Environmental Policy: Trust and the Politics of Implementation*. Washington, D.C.: Georgetown University Press, 2004.

Schmalensee, Richard, and Robert N. Stavins. *The SO_2 Allowance Trading System: The Ironic History of a Grand Policy Experiment*. Cambridge, MA: MIT Center for Energy and Environmental Policy Research, 2012, http://web.mit.edu/ceepr/www/publications/workingpapers/2012-012.pdf.

Selznick, Philip. *TVA and the Grassroots: A Study in the Sociology of Formal Organization*. Berkeley: University of California Press, 1949.

Shapiro, Fred R., ed. *The Yale Book of Quotations*. New Haven, CT: Yale University Press, 2006.

Silver, Nate. *The Signal and the Noise: Why So Many Predictions Fail—But Some Don't*. New York: Penguin, 2012.

Smith, Laurence C. *The World in 2050: Four Forces Shaping Civilization's Northern Future*. New York: Dutton, 2010.

Speth, James G. "The Global 2000 Report and Its Aftermath," in *Foundations of Environmental Sustainability: The Coevolution of Science and Policy*, ed. Larry Rockwood, Ronald E. Stewart, and Thomas Dietz. New York: Oxford University Press, 2008, 47–50.

Stern, David I. "The Rise and Fall of the Environmental Kuznets Curve." *World Development* 32, no. 8 (2004): 1419–1439.

Steward, David R., Paul J. Bruss, Xiaoying Yang, Scott A. Staggenborg, Stephen M. Welch, and Michael D. Apley. "Tapping Unsustainable Groundwater Stores for Agricultural Production in the High Plains Aquifer of Kansas, Projections to 2110." *Proceedings of the National Academy of Sciences* 110, no. 37 (2013): E3477–E3486.

Teixeira, Ruy, ed. *Red, Blue and Purple America: The Future of Election Demographics.* Washington, D.C.: Brookings, 2008.

Tetlock, Phillip E. *Expert Political Judgment: How Good is it? How Can we Know?* Princeton, NJ: Princeton University Press, 2006.

Tompkins, Jonathan R. *Organization Theory and Public Management.* Belmont, CA: Thomson Wadsworth, 2005.

Toner, Robin. "Bush, in Enemy Waters, Says Rival Hindered Cleanup of Boston Harbor." *New York Times,* September 2, 1988, http://www.nytimes.com/1988/09/02/us/bush-in-enemy-waters-says-rival-hindered-cleanup-of-boston-harbor.html.

Train, Russell E. *Politics, Pollution, and Pandas: An Environmental Memoir.* Washington, D.C.: Shearwater, 2003.

United Nations World Commission on Environment and Development. *Our Common Future.* New York: Oxford University Press, 1987.

Vig, Norman J. "Presidential Leadership and the Environment," in *Environmental Policy: New Directions for the Twenty-First Century,* 8th ed., ed. Norman J. Vig and Michael E. Kraft. Thousand Oaks, CA: CQ Press, 2013, 84–108.

Vig, Norman J., and Michael E. Kraft, eds. *Environmental Policy: New Directions for the Twenty-First Century,* 8th ed. Washington, D.C.: CQ Press, 2012.

Vig, Norman J., and Michael E. Kraft. "Appendix 2," in *Environmental Policy: New Directions for the Twenty-First Century,* 8th ed., ed. Norman J. Vig and Michael E. Kraft. Thousand Oaks, CA: CQ Press, 2013, 404.

Wicker, Tom. *One of Us: Richard Nixon and the American Dream.* New York: Random House, 1991.

Wilford, John Noble. "On Hand for Space History as Superpowers Spar." *New York Times,* July 14, 2009, http://www.nytimes.com/2009/07/14/science/space/14mission.html?emc=eta1.

Williams, Dennis C. "The Guardian: EPA's Formative Years, 1970–1973." EPA Doc. No. 202-K-93-002 (September 1993), http://www2.epa.gov/aboutepa/guardian-epas-formative-years-1970-1973.

Wilson, James Q. *Bureaucracy: What Government Agencies Do and Why They Do It.* New York: Basic Books, 1989.

Wilson, Woodrow. "The Study of Administration." *Political Science Quarterly* 2, no. 2 (1887): 197–222.

Wlezien, Christopher. "Patterns of Representation: Dynamics of Public Preferences and Policy." *Journal of Politics* 66, no. 1 (2004): 1–24.

Wlezien, Christopher. "The Public as Thermostat: Dynamics of Preferences for Spending." *American Journal of Political Science* 39, no. 4 (1995): 981–1000.

Wlezien, Christopher, and Stuart N. Soroka. "Measures and Models of Budgetary Policy." *Policy Studies Journal* 31, no. 2 (2003): 273–386.

Young, Don. "Obama's EPA as an Employment Prevention Agency." *Politico,* March 15, 2012, http://www.politico.com/news/stories/0312/74072.html.

INDEX